Ms. Clarice —
  We are sorry,
and trust you.
Our love and prayers are with you —
"Mr. George"   12-26-03

Reflections

by

Earline Ross Cole

Earline Ross Cole

Philippians 1:3

With Love + Appreciation
to "Mr. George" + "Ms. Clarice"
Thank you for your kind
Remarks concerning "Reflections"
in the Houston Home Journal —
your interest in the Column
is most encouraging.
You are a source of inspiration
to all whose lives you touch.
It was nice to have you
join the Governor —
  memories with
    BVMC friends —
      12-11-03
        E.C.

Published by

IN HIS STEPS PUBLISHING
P.O. Box 3563
Macon, Georgia 31205-3563

Printed in the United States of America
© 2003 by Earline Ross Cole
ALL RIGHTS RESERVED!

ISBN: 1-58535-078-8

INTRODUCTION

Earline Ross Cole has a most unique and refreshing outlook on life. On the following pages you will find her keen insights on the most ordinary of situations. Her observations and interpretations will leave you both humored and challenged. She brings her well earned wisdom to bear on the simplest things of life and gives us a glimpse of living from her distinct perspective.

We all have so much to learn, and Earline illustrates these important life lessons from the commonplace. She teaches us that there is so much wisdom available, if we will just open our eyes and see. We are reminded that the very best lessons are not learned in ivy-coated libraries, and that formal education and world travel are not prerequisites to wisdom. The true lessons are in the stuff of life. They happen when we least expect it. She reminds us to always be watching and learning, especially from the mouths of babes. Her writing is fresh, personal, and it reflects her deep and abiding faith in God. This book, just like her life, is dedicated to the Glory of God.

I know that each of you who reads this book will enjoy it as much as I have. I know that you will be all the richer having benefited from her writings.

Grace & Peace,

Bill Woodson, Pastor
Bonaire United Methodist Church
Bonaire, Georgia

ACKNOWLEDGMENTS

God has richly blessed me with a family who knows the meaning and importance of love. Appreciation is expressed from the depth of my heart to each one within our family circle who provides prayerful encouragement for all of my endeavors.

Special love is directed to those precious little ones and wonderful youths used of God to teach through their innocence and sincerity. Since the first edition of "Led By A Child" most of the youngsters who inspired the little lessons have reached maturity, some of whom are now parents being taught little lessons by children of their own.

To the Houston Home Journal, I am grateful for the privilege and honor of submitting weekly columns from the past which appear under the heading of *"Reflections"*.

My sincere thanks to the Bonaire United Methodist Women for accepting this publication as a means of securing funds for the Bonaire United Methodist Church Outreach Ministry. Also, to Nancy Jackson, Sunday School teacher who, in one lesson stated, "If you have a good idea, do something about it!" And to Dr. H. Cullen Talton, III for his support to this, and many other outreach services of the Bonaire United Methodist Women.

Thanks to John Holsenbeck for original illustrations and to Alana Carter for her devotion to proof reading and researching selected scripture verses. Both are eighth-grade students at Bonaire Middle High School.

Above all, I am grateful to God, Who is The Author, for granting me the privilege of writing and compiling brief devotionals to share.

Earline Ross Cole
Summer, 2003

DEDICATION

Reflections is dedicated first of all to God, then, to the two grandsons and a "tribe" of nieces, nephews, great-nieces, great-nephews and great-greats. God has placed these within our family circle to be loved and nurtured into the circle of His family.

Also, I am dedicating this work to "Grandpa"/ "Papas", whose shoes are rapidly being filled by our grandsons.

Grandma Cole
a.k.a. "E-Maw"

Grandson Update:
Doug Cole has completed his freshman year at Andrew College, Cuthbert, Georgia.
Ben Carter is a senior at Warner Robins High School, Warner Robins, Georgia.

Contents

Introduction	3
Acknowledgments	4
Dedication	5
Preface	11

<u>Chapter One</u>

"Led By A Child"	13
Earline Ross Cole	14
Always Someone Near	16
Seek The Light	17
Loving Arms Comfort	18
Be Receptive To Help	19
Beginning of Golf Course	20
Jesus Loves Me, Too!	21
Something For Jesus	22
Definite Place of Belonging	23
Rewarded Accordingly	24
Listen and Learn	25
"MayI?"	26
Work From Bottom To Top	27
Share The Spotlight	28
Something Out Of Nothing	29
Lad Soothed By Teacher's Kindness	30
Worthless Item Prompts Worthwhile Reminder	31
Bite Your Tongue	32
True Identity	33
Magic Word	34

We Are Never Alone	35
I Got One!	36
You Gotta Ask	37
Just Come'd On In	38
Control To Comfort	39
Seven Alone	40
Owe No Man!	41
People Are People	42
Try Kindness	43
Show and Tell	44
Seek The Giver	45
Out On A Limb	46
Making The Right Move	47
What A Way To Start A Day!	48
Honesty Is Best Policy	49
Finding Time For Wants	50
Gifted With Loving Nature	51
Use Faith	52
Man With The Plan	53
Never Out Of God's Sight	54
Three Little Words	55
Do's and Don'ts	56
Memory of Faded Flower	57
Teacher's Love Follows Student	58
Where To Stop and Rest	59
Young Friends Fill Deficiency	60
Little Guy Accepts Why	61
Bouquet Conveys Love	62
Good Little Bad Boy	63

Search For Meaningful Life	64
Is It Important?	65
Reaching For The Forbidden	66
Each Will Receive Reward	67
Prayer Of Mind and Heart	68
Love Made Difference	69
Look For An Excuse To Praise	70
Spread Love Along Life's Highway	71
Bubble Gum Giver	72
Smiles Reveal Gladness From Within	73
Looking Out For Another	74
Singing Stops Sobbing	75
Something New	76
Closer Look Helps Vision	77
Grabbing For Cookies	78
True Friend's Door Remains Open	79
Identity Should Be No Problem	80
Rusty Heels Insignificant	81
Lot To Be Learned From Children	82
No Bargains Or Threats	83
Now, That's Nice!	84
Not Perfect, Just Forgiven!	85
Qualities Developed Through Lifestyles	86
Each One Capable	87
Wiggling Clear of God's Hand	88
'Cause His Hand Is Bigger Than Mine!	89
Stay Spiritually Connected	90
Premature 'A-Men' Is Like Putting Cart Before Horse	91

Come As A Little Child Unto The Lord	92

Chapter Two
Selected From Files	93
Letting Go Of Hurt	94
Not Enough Good Said	95
Perfect Pattern Taking Shape	97
Just Read The Directions	98
Share The Sunshine Of God's Love	99
We Break Things, But God Fixes	100

Chapter Three
Halloween	101
Door Opened To Treat	102
Closely Watched	103
Polly Punkin-Head's Purpose	104
Spooky's First Halloween	105
Who's Behind That Mask?	106
Letter To Young Friends: October 1982	107

Chapter Four
The Greatest Of These Is Love	109
Examination of Love	110
Love - In School Traffic	112
More Than Coincidence	114
"Miss Lizzie"	115
Barking Up The Wrong Tree	116
Time Heals All Wounds?	117
From My Heart To Yours	119

PREFACE
By Rev. Donald E. Cole

"At that time the disciples came to Jesus, saying, "Who then is greatest in the kingdom of heaven?" And He called a child to Himself and set him before them and said, 'Truly I say to you, unless you are converted and become like children, you shall not enter the kingdom of heaven. Whoever then humbles himself as this child, he is the greatest in the kingdom of heaven.'"
(Matthew 18:1-4 NAS)

We live in a day where it seems that everyone is seeking power, status, wealth, and control. Business executives drive "power" cars, go out to "power" lunches, and even have consultants to advise them on "power" colors in the clothes they wear. This is not new at all. We see that even the disciples were asking about the power, status, and control in their day. Isn't it interesting that Jesus answered their question about the most powerful by placing a little child before them? "Whoever humbles himself as this child is the greatest in the kingdom of heaven." Somehow that just doesn't seem to fit with our picture of a "powerful" leader, does it?

This book includes a collection of little lessons about children. As you read these lessons you will see the characteristics of simple honesty, humility, trust, and yes, even leadership, that Jesus said was necessary to enter the kingdom of heaven. These little lessons, and additional material, were written and compiled in this book with the hope that you will smile, laugh, and perhaps even cry, but most of all that you will discover the simple truths of God reflected in the life of a child. When we find that truth we discover that we have been truly, **"Led By A Child."**

Chapter One

"Led By A Child"

**From *"Led By A Child"*
Published 1991**

Earline Ross Cole

Accounts given in *Led By A Child* are all inspired by children. All were selected from Little Lessons, an inspirational column written by Earline Ross Cole which originated in 1976 and was a regular feature in several weekly Georgia newspapers in Houston, Bibb, Wilkinson and Lamar Counties.

Putting her writing aside to pursue other interests, Earline's last Little Lesson was published in 1992.

On June 28, 2003 her column was revived under the heading of *Reflections*, and appears in the Spiritual Growth section of The Houston Home Journal's weekend edition.

Born on December 27, 1930 in Milner, Georgia, Earline entered first grade at Milner High School, Lamar County, Georgia where she graduated from the eleventh grade in 1948.

Robert Brown Cole and Mary Earline Ross were married on July 4, 1948. Honorably discharged from the United States Army, Robert retired from Civil Service employment at Robins Air Force Base, Warner Robins, Georgia in 1980.

The Houston County couple have two children. Their son, The Reverend Donald E. Cole and his wife Leslie, have one son - Doug Cole. The family resides in Albany, Georgia. Donald is an ordained Baptist minister and is principal consultant for a management consulting firm.

The Coles' daughter, Linda Carter, holds a secretarial position at Robins Air Force Base. She, her husband

Bobby and their son, Ben reside in Bonaire, Georgia.

Making her profession of faith at the age of 12 in the Milner Baptist Church, Earline later transferred to her husband's denomination. Both have been active members of the Bonaire United Methodist Church since 1954. Placing no emphasis on denomination, they prefer to be recognized simply as "Christians."

Writing has come to be a form of personal witness for Earline Ross Cole. She seeks no recognition for herself, but strives towards portraying Christ as the center of life.

Her inspirational column, *Reflections*, illustrates how God can be seen, heard and felt through daily experiences.

This printing of *Led By A Child* contains her series of Halloween articles reflecting "little lessons" portrayed through annual visits from neighborhood children. Other selected articles are also included.

Always Someone Near

Many reminders come to us through observing babies as they progress through the developmental stages of life. The little one who is beginning to pull up, looses its balance. Experiencing a fall, the infant is alarmed and begins to cry. Promptly someone who loves, cares and understands comes to the rescue. Being comforted and reassured, the infant proceeds to pull itself up.

Eventually, the child takes its first steps while holding to something or someone for support. Then, after taking that first step and learning to "walk alone", the child becomes more independent. Experiencing more falls along the way, the little one soon learns that there are times when the cry goes unheard by a human ear. No one comes to comfort.

As progression is made from childhood to youth, there will possibly be moments of doubt as to whether or not anyone cares. These doubts are subject to remain until progression from human dependency to depending on God has been achieved.

At this point comes the realization that we always have Someone near Who loves, cares and understands. No cry goes unheard - we never walk alone!

"And He said, My presence shall go with thee, and I will give thee rest." (Exodus 33:14)

Seek The Light

A sleepy-headed little fellow played in a secluded room where a pad had been placed on the floor for nap time. Doors were closed and room darkened in an attempt to encourage the little one to settle down. Light from an adjoining room attracted the little fellow's attention. Energetically crawling away from the darkened area, he headed towards the light.

The little fellow's action exemplifies the direction we should seek to follow through life. We need not be confined to a world of darkness when the light of life shines through as a beacon to guide us.

This assurance He has given: *"I am the light of the world; he that followeth me shall not walk in darkness, but shall have the light of life."* (John 8:12)

Loving Arms Comfort

Caught up in tiresome activities among a multitude of people, a little toddler was tuckered out near the end of a long day. Expecting comfort, he reached up to his father. Crying, he begged, "Take me, take me!" The plea was acknowledged by the father who placed his hand upon the youngster's head.

More than a touch was needed by the child who continued to cry, "Take me, take me!" Fortunately, a sympathetic mother realized the need for and provided the love and attention which was so desperately being sought.

Perhaps a situation of this sort is basis for the slogan, "God couldn't be everywhere so He created mothers." However, we know that God can be and is everywhere. Had He not been on the scene, most likely, the exhausted mother would not have shown compassion.

As children of God, we can depend on Him to hear our pleas when we cry, "Take me, take me!" A touch of His hand should suffice, but there are times when we feel the need for more. At such times our Father takes us lovingly in His arms and carries us until we are rested enough to once again walk by His side.

"The eternal God is our dwelling place and underneath are the everlasting arms." (Deuteronomy 33:27a RSV)

Be Receptive To Help

A blank shot was fired into the air and the race was on. Nearby, ready to give help to anyone who might "run into trouble," was a Rescue Mission attendant.

As the runners made their way along the designated three-mile route, one lad suffered a fall. His being ahead of a group of participants made it possible for him to gain control over the situation and get back in the running.

Rejoining the racers, the youngster courageously commented, "There's no use starting something if you don't finish!" Making his way down a steep hill, his foot slipped. Down he went for a second time. Not to be defeated, he brushed himself off and insisted, "I think I can make it . . . I'll try!"

With little persuasion from the compassionate Rescue Mission attendant, the determined lad agreed to taking another break. Bless his heart, it seemed not to be his day for running, but unknown to him, he was being used in a special way by portraying a valuable lesson in life. We must be willing to put forth our best effort. We must also be willing to admit a need for and be receptive to help.

Whatever the challenge, as we go forth with the attitude of the young racer, there is always a Compassionate Attendant nearby who will help us reach our goal. No doubt, He was instrumental in a determined little fellow crossing the finish line and receiving his reward.

"Be not thou far from me, O Lord: O my strength, haste thee to help me." (Psalms 22:19)

Beginning of Golf Course

Starting points. Whatever we do and whatever we become depends to a large degree on the kind of attitude we develop at the starting point.

A youngster greeted an adult visitor in his home with an enthusiastic, "Do you 'wanna' play golf?"

Noticing mounds of dirt from yardwork done by the lad's father, the visitor asked, "Do you have a golf course?"

"No," replied the youngster, "But I have a hole!"

The youngster's attitude was a healthy one for his age. His was an optimistic outlook that pushed aside the negative. He didn't have a golf course, but he had the beginnings of one. Making the most of what he had, the lad wasn't held back or discouraged by what he didn't have. He was ready to play golf. But, as time goes by and the youngster advances to maturity, he will realize that it takes more than "one-hole-golf" to really play the game!

Going from start to finish takes desire and determination. It takes a combination of time, talents and money. It takes personal sacrifices and the willingness to accomplish the goal, barring all discouraging obstacles.

"Be of good courage, and He shall strengthen your heart, all ye that hope in the Lord." (Psalms 31:24)

Jesus Loves Me, Too!

"As for us, the love of God was revealed by the fact that God sent His only Son into the world, that through Him we might live." (I John 4:9, Modern)

"Jesus loves me this I know, For the Bible tells me so. Little ones to Him belong, They are weak but He is strong."

As the little girl joyfully sang of Jesus' love, her younger brother went about play.

"Yes, Jesus loves me. Yes, Jesus loves me. Yes, Jesus loves me, The Bible tells me so," his sister sang.

He didn't sing along, but when the song ended the little brother chimed in to support the well-known lyrics.

"Jesus loves me, too, don't He, Mama?", the little fellow asked, turning to his mother to confirm that, "Jesus loves me, this I know" was meant for him, too.

Many songs have been written expressing the love of Jesus for His "little ones." Those songs of assurance were written for the young and the old.

Not everyone can sing. Not everyone attempts to sing. But, we can all be attentive to the meaningful words of songs that tell of the love Jesus has for us. And we can each experience the feeling of security as did one so young, and echo out: "Jesus loves me, too!"

Something For Jesus

"The love of Christ controls us." (II Corinthians 5:14, RSV)

Every time I see a roly-poly bug, I am reminded of a very sweet incident that was shared by a grandmother.

Three-year old Billy and his younger brother were keeping themselves entertained with the fascinating little bugs one Sunday morning. As grandmother gathered the two boys up for Sunday School, they willingly released and left behind the bugs which had kept them occupied. At least grandmother thought so.

Before entering the sanctuary, little Billy looked up, opened his hand and said to his grandmother, "I'm going to show Jesus my roly-poly."

Not every child would have wanted to be taken away from play and carried to church. But little Billy, being one of many youngsters who has learned to associate church with Jesus, wanted to go and wanted to share.

I once heard a message based on the question, "What do You Have In Your Hand?"

A roly-poly might sound insignificant, but imagine how happy Jesus must have felt to have been remembered in such a sweet and loving way by a young lad.

Definite Place of Belonging

"And now just as you trusted Christ to save you, trust Him, too for each day's problems; live in vital union with Him." (Colossians 2:6, Living Bible)

A fifth-grade student shared an experience with a difficult math problem. The problem itself wasn't so difficult but getting the right answer was. Dealing with decimals can be a frustrating experience. But, through all the trials and errors, the student did not permit herself to become frustrated. With patience and determination, she stuck with the problem until discovering the solution.

Putting the decimal in the wrong place was the cause of the student's difficulty. That one little dot . . . the "powerful decimal," it was named . . . had created all sorts of confusion. Once the error was recognized, the right answer to the problem was found and the student was better prepared to deal with others that followed.

How well we can relate to the math problem and the solution. In this great universe, we, like the "powerful decimal," have a definite place of belonging.

Being just a tiny bit out of place can create confusion. But, when we are in place, according to God's plan, we discover solutions to problems which once seemed difficult and are better prepared to deal with those that follow.

Rewarded Accordingly

Called to the door by a gentle knock, I found two little girls waiting expectantly.

"Would you like to buy some Girl Scout cookies?", the Brownie Scout politely asked.

"Honey, we've already bought cookies," I explained. "Be sure to get to me first next year, O.K.?"

"O.K.", she replied, and like a genuine Girl Scout, thanked me and then added, "Have a good day."

Well, I could not let it go at that. Later, two telephone orders for two more boxes of cookies were placed with two ambitious little girls.

Having been a Girl Scout leader, I haven't forgotten how hard some troop members worked towards meeting requirements to earn a special reward for selling cookies. I haven't forgotten the commendable and appreciated adult support which boosted sales. Neither have I forgotten the few girls, strictly on their own, whose contacts were limited. Because of their situations, it seemed unfair that they should be excluded from receiving an award when they, too, had applied their best efforts.

Discussion of policies related to the annual fund raising project resulted in the birth of an idea. Girls who had better opportunities to make contacts agreed to lend helping hands to their sister scouts. When one had sold her quota, additional sales were accredited to another who was "doing her best." When time came to hand out awards, there was not one little girl who was undeserving of the award received!

In addition to meeting individual quotas, 100 percent bonds of friendship were strengthened and the toop surpassed its goal.

No doubt there would be some disagreement over the approach used, but I have no regrets. We do not have equal opportunities in all areas, but thank God, our final reward will not be based on competiveness. God desires that we do our best in service sincerely given for Him.

"He that planteth and he that watereth are one: and every man shall receive his own reward according to his own labor." (I Corinthians 3:8)

Listen and Learn

A youngster was asked if he liked school. "No," he honestly replied.

"Then how do you learn?", he was further questioned. To the latter inquiry he responded, "I listen."

The lad is on the right track. So often knowledge is lost simply because the subject is not of interest to the student. Willingness and desire to learn make it possible to conquer obstacles that might otherwise hold us back.

"Listen to advice and accept instruction, that you may gain wisdom for the future", are the words recorded in Proverbs 19:20, Revised Standard Version, RSV.

A good example is portrayed by the youngster who, although he didn't like school, was willing to listen in order to learn.

As students of life, we are each confronted with situations we might choose to avoid. While we do not always like the subjects we are dealing with, we can learn to cope with them and gain wisdom in the process.

"May I?"

A group of youngsters were involved in the familiar game, "May I?" Given instructions to "take a giant step," one child inquired, "May I?"

"Yes, you may," the leader replied. Thus advancement was made.

As the game continued, members of the group progressed towards the goal. Occasionally however, advancement was hindered for those who failed to secure permission to move forward.

"Take a baby step," one child was instructed. The step was taken. "Go back," he was then told, "You didn't say, 'May I?'"

Reflecting on the game and its connection with everyday living, we realize that even a "baby step" taken out of order can prove to be a hindrance.

We have a leader to direct our steps. How much better life could be for those of us who sometimes have to back up and start over.

To remove any trace of doubt as to whether or not we are taking the right step in the right direction at the right time, we need only to inquire, "Father, May I?"

"The steps of a good man are directed by the Lord. He delights in each step they take." (Psalms 37:23, Living Bible)

Work From Bottom To Top

James, an independent youngster, was in the process of getting himself dressed. He was progressing nicely until stumped by buttoning his shirt. With great patience he buttoned from top to bottom only to discover an extra button at the bottom and an extra buttonhole at the top.

Not to be defeated, the youngster unbuttoned his shirt and repeated the procedure, getting the same results. After several attempts, he was advised to start at the bottom and "button up" his shirt.

Willingly following the advice, he was pleased over the accomplishment when he reached the top.

Through his trial and error attempts, Little James adequately illustrated a typical difficulty experienced by striving towards instant success. Those who attempt to start at the top are likely to find themselves in the position of having to start all over, and work from the bottom to reach the top.

Paul's confession in Philippians 3:12 suggests his lifestyle to have been based on the "Button Up" theory: *"I don't mean to say I am perfect,"* he admitted, *"I haven't learned all I should even yet, but I keep working toward that day when I will finally be all that Christ saved me for and wants me to be."* (Living Bible)

Share The Spotlight

The young man was being interviewed concerning accomplishments achieved through the use of a special talent. As the interview progressed, he broke from giving answers, suggesting an interview with a friend who had won numerous awards in the same category. Although he was appreciative of the recognition being received, the unselfish young man desired to share the spotlight with a deserving friend.

His thoughtfulness reveals a higher accomplishment achieved through Christian maturity. Not everyone would be humbled to the point of sharing the spotlight with another when personal attention is being attained. The commendable attitude of this young man is a sign of sincere Christianity.

Would not our world be a better place with more people sharing their spotlights?

"No one should be looking out for his own interests, but for the interests of others." (I Corinthians 10:24, TEV)

Something Out Of Nothing

As a special project, a group of youngsters was given the assignment of making something out of nothing. Each child was given the responsibility of deciding what to make and what would be used in the making.

Within the group was a little girl who chose to make her creation from red clay. Adding water to this clay, she stirred until the mixture was the right consistency. With the idea that she had nothing more than a pan full of red clay from the earth to begin with, she carefully molded a dish for her project.

Starting with "nothing", she created "something" of usefulness. We might choose to compare ourselves with the child's creation.

What were we to begin with? What did we become? Did God create something useful out of nothing when He molded us?

"But now, O Lord, thou art our Father; we are the clay, and thou our potter; and we all are the work of thy hand." (Isaiah 64:8)

Lad Soothed By Teacher's Kindness

A small lad in school, head close to his desk, thinking, figuring. His brow perspires, his face is worried, as he is a conscientious little man of nine years. The answer won't come. He cannot seem to get it right, no matter how hard he tries.

Soon the teacher comes and sits beside him in his desk. He is a bit nervous to have her so near. The concern for the lad's problem and the teacher's gentleness and kindness puts him at ease. The teacher helps the lad to think. He finds the solution.

The teacher did not do the problem. She did better than that. She soothed the troubled lad with kindness and gently persuaded him to find the correct answer for himself.

We have many school teachers like unto the one previously mentioned. The teachers lead, guide and direct young lives and help them to find the right solutions to many of life's problems. Their wisdom reminds me of a favorite scripture in James 3:17:

"Wisdom from above is first pure, then peaceful, gentle and easy to be entreated, full of mercy and good fruits."

(Contributed by Sarah Conley)

Worthless Item Prompts Worthwhile Reminder

A young girl turned to an adult for guidance with a problem. It seemed she had "lost" something of personal value and had seen a friend with an identical item.

The child believed to have the misplaced item was called to one side where she listened to the other explain her dilemma.

When the case had been stated, the suspicious youngster implied, "And you have one just like it."

Without any disagreement, the friend handed the "lost" item to its rightful owner. The item in question could not have been worth more than a nickel, but through the incident comes a worthwhile reminder - a beautiful illustration from Matthew 5:9:

"Blessed are the peacemakers: for they shall be called the children of God."

Bite Your Tongue

The little girl thinks she has a serious problem. "I bite my tongue all the time," she said, and "I do it on purpose." She doesn't know why the habit was developed. It's just one of those senseless habits with no logical explanation. The habit could be painful and even cause real complications, but is not that severe.

When the child mentioned the peculiar practice of biting her tongue, the thought automatically came to my mind that perhaps it is not as senseless as might be assumed.

The idiom, Bite your tongue, a reminder that some things are best left unsaid, has been around for a long time. On occasions when thoughts ought not to be verbalized, but the temptation to express a needless opinion becomes strong, it would be beneficial to bite the tongue.

Repeating rumors seldom serve any worthwhile purpose. Rather than circulate ungrounded information, biting the tongue would pay off.

Inconsiderate remarks, as having been proven, are damaging. To avoid saying something regretful that would hurt another, bite the tongue.

"He who wants to enjoy life and see happy days must keep his tongue from speaking evil and his life from uttering deceit." (I Peter 3:10, Modern)

True Identity

"I know my own and my own know me." (John 10:14, RSV)

Some years ago our family served as a foster home for children in our county. Reasons for our visitors being with us were not revealed. We only knew there was a need to be met and we were fortunate in being available to fill the need.

Quite a few infants passed through our arms. For each one there remains a special place in our hearts.

Most of "our babies" were with us only a short period. The longest visit was made by a little girl eight weeks of age when she came to us.

Growing into a "toddler", hearing our own off-springs call us "Mama" and "Daddy", it was natural that she also recognized us in the same way.

Being in our home for more than a year and treated like a member of the family, it was next to impossible to help one of such tender age make the distinction between her parents and foster parents.

After her return home, the child's parents were kind enough to remain friends with us. We soon lost the Mama and Daddy image as the real Mama and Daddy gained true identity.

A similar situation is true in our relationship with God. We belong to Him, yet it takes awhile for us to learn that He is our Father.

Magic Word

Two-year old Anita had caught on to the significance of the magic word - "Please." The cunning little miss soon became aware that by adding the magic word, her requests were more likely to be granted.

Jimmy was another youngster who applied the magic word with confidence. Scurrying towards the door while glancing over his shoulder, Jimmy pleaded: "Mother, may I go over to Mike's house? Please . . . Mother . . . Please?"

Being a wise little fellow, Jimmy knew to heed his mother's instructions if she said "No." But expecting her approval, he was headed in the direction of Mike's house while asking permission.

The respect and faith exemplified through these childlike illustrations are parallel to that of the Christian in relationship to God. As respecters of God's authority, we should be willing to accept His answer of "No." Still we can have confidence in knowing He will approve when we seek His permission for things which will not prove to be harmful.

"And we are sure of this, that He will listen to us whenever we ask Him for anything in line with His will. And if we really know He is listening when we talk to Him and make our requests, then we can be sure that He will answer us." (I John 5:14-15, Living Bible)

Out of common courtesy, we might want to give thought to applying that magic word, "Please," when we express our desires to God.

We Are Never Alone

Thunder roared . . . lightning flashed . . . a little dog trembled with fear.

"Why is he shaking?" a youngster asked his grandmother. Explaining to the child that the little dog was afraid, she asked if he feared the lightning and thunder.

"No," the child replied, "because Jesus said, 'Don't be afraid, I am with you always.'"

Always! That means forever! And the little fellow was right. No matter where we are or what we are doing, we are never alone. God is right there with us.

Most of us, like the little dog, become afraid at times. God understands our fears, but He wants us to have faith in Him like the little child and trust Him to take care of us. Psalms 23:4b is a good verse to remember when fear creeps into our minds:

"I will fear no evil; for Thou art with me."

I Got One!

"Papa Jim" baited the hook for his five-year-old grandson, Wayne. Just as soon as the baited hook sank beneath the water he got a bite. With "Papa Jim's" assistance, Wayne successfully landed his catch. It was a big one, too!

Such excitement I had never seen. The little fellow was so thrilled, he jumped up and down clapping his hands and repeatedly shouting . . . "I got one . . . I got one!"

That was Wayne's first catch, but I've got a feeling that young man is on his way to becoming an enthusiastic fisherman.

Not everyone is interested in recreational fishing, but we each have the opportunity to become "fishers of men."

In Mark 1:17, Jesus said: *"Come ye after me, and I will make you to become fishers of men."* As such, we need Wayne's enthusiasm. We should reflect the excitement demonstrated by the five-year-old when he reeled in his first fish. With each "catch" we should be so thrilled we feel like jumping up and down, clapping our hands and shouting . . . "I got one . . . I got one!"

You Gotta Ask

Listening to the voice of one youngster to another outside my kitchen, these words were heard: "If you want some 'tater chips, you gotta ask for them."

The two entered my kitchen, made their requests, and received their "tater chips."

Children are not encouraged to go around asking for "handouts", but this "Little Lesson" has a moral.

God's abounding love is ever present and available. He showers us with blessings without our asking. Still He has promised, *"If ye abide in me, and my words in you, ye shall ask what ye will, and it shall be done unto you."* (John 15:7)

God does not force Himself upon us. If we want Him to fulfill His promise, we must meet the requirements . . .

Abide in Him -- His words in us -- and then -- we "gotta ask Him", not for "tater chips", but for things more essential to our spiritual growth.

Just Come'd On In

One of our young friends came by for a neighborly visit with my husband and me. During conversation she announced, "Me and Tommy come over here 'yest'dy. We knocked and knocked and couldn't get nobody to the door so we just come'd on in."

Talking on, the child said, "We tippy-toed real quiet and saw somebody asleep in bed so we come'd on back out." Without scolding, I talked with our little friend about not entering the home of another unless someone in the home let her in.

The incident brought to mind a little chorus, Open Wide The Door. The chorus goes like this:

Open wide the door - Let the Savior in;
He will gladly enter there
He'll cleanse your heart from sin,
Give new life within
Take away all doubt and care.
But the latch is on the inside,
Won't you draw the bar and open wide
And let the Savior in;
Others you may win - If you will let the Savior in.

Christ wants to enter our hearts, but as the chorus emphasizes, the latch is on the inside. He patiently waits for us to draw the bar and open wide the door.

He does not "just come'd on in", nor does He "tippy-toe real quiet and come'd on back out."

Once we let Christ in, He stays unless we shove Him out!

Control To Comfort

During Christmas holidays, back in 1976, I visited overnight with my brother and his family.

Being accustomed to a bedroom with electric heat, getting comfortable was slightly difficult.

Finally settled down, with a young niece snuggled against my back, I was ready for a "long winter's nap."

The next morning my little "bed-fellow" announced that she was fixing to arise. "Oooooooooooooo, please don't do that, I'll freeze," I pleaded.

Ready to start her day, she insisted on crawling out - but, considerately added, "I'll turn the electric blanket on for you."

"You mean I've been about to freeze all night and have been under an electric blanket all the time?!" I responded.

She laughed, pushed the "control to comfort" and went her merry way.

We Christians often put ourselves in the same position. Needless hours of spiritual discomfort are experienced when the "Control to Comfort" is so near.

Isaiah 55:6 says: *"Seek ye the Lord while He may be found, call ye upon His name while He is near."*

No matter what the situation, Prayer is our "Control to Comfort." God is our Source, but no one else can "push the button" for us!

Seven Alone

Based on a true experience, the movie of the seventies, Seven Alone is a touching one.

Filled with fictitious excitement of a miraculous rescue from every encounter with danger, the real excitement came with the miraculous survival of every dangerous encounter.

Seven Alone could have been a real thriller based on fiction. Old Doc could have concocted a sure cure for blood poison, snapping the father of the seven back to recovery. The same holds true in the mother's case of pneumonia.

It didn't happen that way. On separate occasions, each parent was overcome by the diseases, eventually leaving seven young children alone. Each parent, realizing their nearing departure, talked with the oldest son who appeared to be a "good for nothing" Whipper-Snapper. Placing confidence in this young man, his mother gave him his baby sister to raise as his own, asking that he keep the family together.

Some would question why God took the father and mother away from seven children. This was sad, but the thing to be marveled over was how these seven came through their arduous adventure.

It would seem they should have starved or frozen to death, if not killed by the Indians. As they struggled along, their needs were met in one way or another.

Nearing the end of the movie, when all hope would have been gone, struggling for help, as the big brother fell in the snow -- he called out to God. Lifting his head, he saw the house he was attempting to reach.

The children were taken in and provided the necessities of a comfortable life until conditions were more favorable to complete their journey to a homestead location.

Fiction is not required to produce a "real thriller." What can be more thrilling than to know One who can help us through our hardships no matter how impossible they seem to be.

Confronted with death, both parents reflected the faith of Psalms 48:14: *"For this God is our God for ever and ever; He will be our guide even unto death."*

Faith of a father and mother carried over into the lives of their children. Those seven were not alone . . . God was with them all the way!

Owe No Man!

"You owe me a dime", one young fellow was heard to say. "And you owe me a quarter," another chimed in.

As the quarrel continued, a sensible comment was made by a third spokesman who stated, "I'm going to get me a job and earn my own money."

The boys had no idea of the message being conveyed through their conversation.

The incident brought to mind Paul's advice that we *"owe no man anything, but to love one another."*
(Romans 13:8)

Being in the position of offering assistance to those in need should be considered a privilege rather than a loan.

Freely given, then forgotten, acts of love return when most needed, and least expected.

People Are People

Following the song service of a Homecoming event, two small children approached one of the singers. The older of the two spoke up, "You'll shake her hand, won't you?"

Picking the little one up, the singer gave the child an embrace and commented on her prettiness.

The incident brings to mind feelings I once harbored prior to spiritual growth.

A misconception on my part was that any public figure was of a higher status than me. I refrained from mixing and mingling with those in any role of leadership because I believed them to be superior beings.

Like the little child, I did not expect individuals in the spotlight to stoop to my level.

With spiritual growth came the realization that people are people. As God's love shines, it shines on each individual.

Some of the friendliest folks I have met are among those I would once have shied away from.

There is no place for feelings of inferiority or superiority in the life of a Christian. All are on the same level.

Look down on no one . . . Look up only to God! *"Behold how good and how pleasant it is for brethren to dwell together in unity."* (Psalms 133:1)

Try Kindness

An outstanding characteristic of a young friend of mine is his ability to recognize good features in others and honor them with compliments. During the time of our acquaintance, I have noticed that often, without even realizing it, he has brightened someone's day by words of kindness. Seemingly he meets no strangers.

My young friend's consideration of others reminds me that so often my eyes are blinded to the good qualities of another individual by looking more closely for undesirable qualities.

I am also reminded that my undesirable qualities often overshadow the more pleasant ones, and of the spiritual uplift that an unexpected compliment brings.

Unaware of the direct influence he has been in my life, my young friend's thoughtfulness enforces a "little lesson" taught by my parents which I sometimes fail to remember.

There is no one so bad that some good can not be found. In looking for the good, we help someone else, and at the same time we help ourselves rise to a higher level.

"Human nature" seems to be to latch on to what we do not like in another individual and magnify these qualities. By applying kindness, this thing called "human nature" can be converted.

Paul's advice to the Colossians was this: *"Put on then, as God's chosen ones, holy and beloved, compassion, kindness, lowliness, meekness and patience."* (Colossians 3:12, RSV)

Show And Tell

A small child frequently said to her mother in a quiet and timid manner, "I love you."

Attempting to encourage the youngster to put love in action rather than mere words, time and time again the mother replied, "Don't tell me -- show me!"

Little did the mother realize the inward pain her child felt by having "spoken love" rejected.

Though often treated affectionately, the little girl was penalized in development of self-expression. Fear of having the verbal phrase refused caused feelings of insecurity.

Because of existing love, a favorable parent-child relationship grew into a strong and mature one as the two grew wiser.

Since "Show and Tell" has been introduced as a means of education, the mother has realized that this method also applies within the family unit.

While we do not hear Jesus speaking the words, "I love you," it was He who first demonstrated "Show and Tell."

One of many examples is recorded in Matthew 9:1-3. After showing compassion for the afflicted man through healing, Jesus voiced His love by saying: *"Son, be of good cheer; thy sins be forgiven thee."*

Seek The Giver

Several children were visiting in the home of a neighbor. Passing through the kitchen, the youngsters hesitated, taking invoice of goodies.

Pausing beside the counter, one child gazed wistfully at a jar of candy. As they waited expectantly, one said to the other, "If you want something, you're going to have to ask for it!"

The visit ended with the children going away empty-handed.

Witnessing the incident, the slogan - "Seek the Giver Instead of the Gift" - came to mind.

Had the children sought out the giver rather than the gift, in all probability their visit would have been rewarded.

There is a little lesson in that slogan for each of us. While it is true that God honors our requests, He does not wait for us to ask.

It is doubtful that there is one among us who has never been guilty of seeking something we wanted, when the search should have been for the One who provides.

We do not always get everything we want, but we can be sure our needs will not be neglected when we seek the Giver instead of the gift.

"For whoever would draw near to God must believe that He exists and that He rewards those who seek Him." (Hebrews 11:6)

Out On A Limb

The scene was more than slightly amusing as two rambunctious playmates bounced from one piece of playground equipment to another in a recreational park.

One of the youngsters scampered up the ladder of a "climber" with intentions of dropping from the top to the ground.

Everything went fine until the child was positioned for her act, with no way down except the courageous plunge.

Finding herself "out on a limb" and a bit unsure, the performer began to call, "Grannie, Grannie, come help me!"

The grandmother, who had patiently remained on the sideline, responded to the plea, helping the little girl to safety.

Do we not at times find ourselves in similar situations as a result of rushing into things without giving thought to the outcome?

God grants us the privilege of thinking for ourselves but He does not turn His back on us.

When we reach the point of calling for His help, He hears and responds to our plea, helping us to safety.

"For the Lord is good, and plenteous in mercy unto all men that call upon His name." (Reference in Psalms 86:1-12)

Making The Right Move

A new math problem in the workbook of a second grade student appeared to be complicated. The object of moving dots from one row to the other was to discover whether the two rows would result in an even or odd number. The mystery in solving the puzzle was determining how many dots to move.

Finally the solution was revealed by a teacher who advised, "Move one dot at a time."

Following the teacher's instructions, the student found the problem to be simple rather than complicated.

Like the second grade student with the math problem, we are sometimes inclined to go off in all directions seeking the solution to peace of mind and heart when all we need to do is make the right move.

The Living Bible quotes Jesus as saying to His disciples: *"I am leaving with you a gift - peace of mind and heart! And the peace I give isn't fragile like the peace the world gives."* (John 14:27)

The same peace of mind and heart is just as available to each of us as it was to the early disciples. Often made complicated - yet so simple once we recognize the solution.

What A Way To Start A Day!

On an "off day" from work, my husband started the day as usual by flipping the television on.

Flopping into my easy chair, I hoped he would soon go outside so I could flip the television off - until he came back in to flip it on again!

Not aware of the station or what program was in progress, I began to direct a portion of my divided attention to the "Today Show."

My interest was quickly captured and my undivided attention gained as "so-called" handicaps were shown in action on ski's.

Hubby and I watched with amazement as demonstrations were given by one who was blind, another who had only one leg, and another whose legs were completely paralyzed.

Then came another portion, narrated by one of the disabled demonstrators, in which struggles toward their achievements were included.

Recognizing downfalls as being a part of accomplishments, the narrator emphasized the importance of concentrating on staying up . . . not down.

Following this particular show, Phil Donahue came on, interviewing young people who were living with cancer. Faced with the unpleasant truths of the disease, the youths smilingly talked of coming to grips with their conditions, giving God credit for their progress.

Pictures of health and happiness, they acknowledged help received through the Center of Attitudinal Healing, and shared methods used to overcome discouragement.

Climaxing the program, Phil was presented a colorful tee-shirt featuring a rainbow, suggesting that every dark cloud is overshadowed by brightness and beauty.

While there was an age variation of those on the two programs, Matthew 21:16 (NAB) seemed fitting. *"From the speech of infants and children you have framed a hymn of praise."*

What a way to start a day! Perhaps in the future I will not be so eager to turn the television off until I have seen what it has to offer!

Honesty Is Best Policy

A coin remained on the desk of a teacher for several days. Inquiring of the class, the teacher discovered the money to have been left by a co-worker.

The amount was not much, but some youngster who could think of so many ways to spend five-cents could have easily been tempted to take or claim the nickel.

Having completely forgotten the coin, the rightful owner was much impressed over the children's honesty. Whatever temptations there might have been were overpowered by knowing what was right.

In Paul's ministry, *"honest things, not only in the sight of the Lord, but also in the sight of man,"* were considered to be of value. (Reference in II Corinthians 8:21)

Measuring up to Paul's standard might sound unlikely in this world of temptations, but as demonstrated by a class of elementary students, is not impossible.

Finding Time For Wants

A young friend asked if I had plans to attend a local football game. "No," I replied, "I just don't have time for ballgames."

"If you really wanted to go, you'd find time," was his prompt comeback.

The truth cannot be denied. Other interests hold priority over sports. I tried getting interested in televised games. That fizzled out when I kept rooting for "George" only to discover that George was not on either team. Then when George played in a televised game, guess who was not at home to see the action? Why wasn't I at home? You might have guessed . . . I was involved in something of more personal interest.

My young friend's comment was a most accurate one. We are inclined to devote our time and energies to things which bring personal satisfaction.

God designed each of us with individual likes and dislikes. He is due the honor of our using these characteristics to set forth examples of Christianity.

"Who can put into words the mighty deeds of the Lord?" (Modern) *"Who can praise Him half enough?" Happiness comes to those who are fair to others and are always just and good."* (Living Bible - Psalms 106:2)

Gifted With Loving Nature

"Be ye therefore imitators of God as His beloved children, and walk in love, as Christ also loved us and gave Himself for us." (Ephesians 5:1-2b)

My husband, a brother-in-law and I were enroute to San Antonio, Texas. It was our second day of travel, and a pleasant one, even in 28-degree weather.

Enjoying the view from our camper window, I found it difficult to believe the weather forecast. Stepping outside when we made a breakfast stop for the fellows, I discovered the forecast to be accurate. It was cold!!

As we sat in the restaurant, a precious child and his parents came in. Having a natural love for children made it easy to become acquainted with loving people.

Nine-year old Larry, a gifted child, did not shy away from the introduction. He responded by reaching up and giving me a great big hug.

Leaving the restaurant, I noticed it didn't seem nearly as cold. The warmth of Larry's love had made a tremendous change in the atmosphere. This brought to mind the words of a little chorus which is a reminder that even in winter time, it can be summer in our hearts.

My visit with Larry and his parents was brief. Our paths might never cross again. But, fond memories will linger of a special friend who is indeed GIFTED . . . gifted with a loving nature which is evidently being nurtured by loving parents.

Use Faith

Completing his reading assignment, a student reached the point which required putting answers in writing. Searching in and around his desk, he was unable to find his misplaced pencil.

"How long has it been since you used your pencil?", he was asked.

"Yesterday," came the reply.

"Yesterday!", the teacher exclaimed. "Well, maybe you should use it more often and you wouldn't have to look for it."

Every student knows the basic supplies needed daily, yet there are always some who are without paper, pencils or other necessities.

Is this not typical of those of us who profess to be Christians? Well aware of the importance of faith, prayer, Bible study and other essentials, it is not unusual for the average person to avoid using that which is needed until it becomes a must.

At such times we might ask ourselves, "How long has it been since I have used my faith, prayer, Bible?" or whatever it may be, applying the teacher's advice to the student with the misplaced pencil.

"Let my mouth be filled with thy praise and with thy honor all the day long." (Psalms 71:8)

Man With The Plan

There is nothing unusual about occasional disorder in a classroom. And, there is nothing unusual about disciplinary action becoming necessary at times. As a caution at such times, the suggestion of confrontation with "the man with the plan," restores order.

One student, not familiar with the expression, inquired as to the identity of "the man with the plan." A classmate volunteered an impressive explanation, then added, "But he ain't the one with the BIG plan!"

The student was right. The school principal is not the one with the BIG plan, but his role of authority is an important one. Fulfilling that role, his concern is evidenced through efforts to guide students toward developing honorable characteristics. Sometimes a confrontation is sufficient within itself. At other times stricter action is required. Nevertheless, "the man with the plan" cares about each boy and girl and has their best interest at heart.

As students of life, we need frequent confrontations with "The Man with the BIG plan," knowing that He wants to help us bring out our best qualities. Sometimes we respond to His gentleness. At other times He has to be strict in order to capture our attention. Even so, His BIG plan is based on love: a love so great that He sacrificed His Son to free us from the bonds of sin.

"What happiness for those whose guilt has been forgiven! What joys when sins are covered over! What relief for those who have confessed their sins and God has cleared their record." (Psalms 32:1-2, Living Bible)

Never Out Of God's Sight

"Can't I let you out of my sight for just one minute?!", a desperate mother asked her mischievous child. In what seemed to be one split second, the youngster had taken advantage of not being watched.

No need to go into details. Most adults have experienced or witnessed comparable situations. Putting ourselves in the same position, we might discover having a wee bit in common with the child.

There's no telling what kind of mischief we children of God would get into were it not for His watchfulness. Temptations are likely to become stronger when we disregard the fact that He never takes His eyes off us.

"I will instruct you and train you in the way you should go; I will counsel you with my eye on you," we are assured in Psalms 32:8 (Modern).

It is for our own protection that we are never out of God's sight. Not even for one split second!

Three Little Words

A treasured note I have kept since 1965 opens with those three little words, "I love you." Written by a child, of her own accord, the simple note offers sincere apology for a mistake. Along with the apology was a promise never to "do it again."

The note has been kept because of my being touched by the love and thoughtfulness of one so young who expressed love, regret and desire not to repeat her error. No longer a little girl, the one who wrote and signed the note, "Your Friend" is one of the sweetest and most trustworthy young ladies I have ever known. Through the years the love has grown stronger . . . the friendship matured. Though our paths seldom cross, our relationship is a lasting and special one founded on those three little words, "I love you."

"Dear friends, let us practice loving each other, for love comes from God and those who are loving and kind show that they are the children of God, and that they are getting to know Him better." (I John 4:7, Living Bible)

Do's And Don'ts

During a visit in our home, a great nephew found himself continuously being cautioned . . . **"DON'T!"** To distract his attention from things which were off limits, he had been provided with toys and gadgets and shown where he could freely play. Exploring the surroundings, the little fellow became interested in a particular object. Remembering to examine with eyes only, he wisely inquired, "What's that, Uncle Robert . . . A Don't?"

On another occasion, while visiting in our home, an energetic youngster was slowed down by a fly-swatter which dangled from a string around my neck. Proving his ability to distinguish between the "Do's and Don'ts", our young visitor was spared a certain amount of discipline.

Adults, like children, are exposed to comparable situations. Living in a world of "Do's and Don'ts" we must carefully choose that which is permissible. As we make our choices, we know to expect discipline from the One who created us. But, isn't it wonderful to know that God grants us more freedom than my little visitors were allowed! Isn't it wonderful that He does not follow us around with a fly-swatter dangling around His neck ready to whack us each time we get out of line?

If He were such a God, I suspect it would take something stronger than a fly-swatter to get my attention at times. Isn't it wonderful that God is of a patient, loving, understanding and forgiving nature as we learn to distinguish between the "Do's and Don'ts" of life?

"The Lord is good; His mercy is everlasting; and His truth endureth to all generations." (Psalms 100:5)

Memory Of Faded Flower

Years ago I watched the one and only bud on a plant in my yard as it developed to maturity. Thinking it would last longer on the bush, I chose not to cut the bloom. For several days the bush of greenery was highlighted by the blossom. And, Oh, it was one of the prettiest I had ever seen because it was the first time the plant had produced a bloom! I wanted it to last forever.

But, along came a precious little girl. Seeing the flower, she picked and brought it to me. Looking innocently up to me, the youngster lovingly said, "I brought you a flower."

The love of that child magnified the beauty of a "lonesome" flower which soon faded and was thrown out. The memory of a little girl with silky, blonde hair, holding a blossom that matched her sparkling blue eyes however, remains in my thoughts.

Never had the flower looked so lovely. And, I'm not so sure that it didn't last as long in the glass of water as it would have on the bush!

Bringing forth more blossoms throughout the years, the bush became symbolic of Romans 13:10 (RSV) as expressed through the actions of a child: *"Love does no wrong to a neighbor, therefore love is the fulfilling of the law."*

Teacher's Love Follows Student

Out of the clear blue, a student asked her teacher, "Do you trust us?" Without hesitating, the teacher replied, "Of course I trust you until you give me reason not to."

While there are some youngsters who do not realize the value of being trusted, the majority are not likely to betray the teacher whose confidence is made known to the students. And, at times, a loving teacher can encourage an untrustworthy student to develop honorable characteristics. Though efforts are not always successful, the concerned teacher does not give up hope. That teacher's love follows her students on their journey through life.

One of the rewards of a dedicated teacher often comes years later when approached by an unrecognized adult who respectfully asks, "Remember me?" Then after renewing the acquaintance, adds, "Thank you for not giving up on me."

This brings to mind a story that is told of a missing watch. A store manager, whose watch had disappeared, notified jewelry dealers in the area. Giving a description of his watch, he asked to be informed in event it turned up. Shortly afterwards the owner of the stolen watch was contacted. The person who carried the watch to the jewelry store was identified.

Confronting the guilty party, the watch owner advised him to get the watch and return it. It was returned without delay and the price one has to pay for committing crime thoroughly explained to the offender.

As the story goes, the "thief" made an all-out effort to prove himself trustworthy to the one who had been his friend.

Applying the illustration to our spiritual lives, we might ask God, "Do you trust us?", to which He will reply, "Of course I trust you." Then, when we find ourselves in situations where we know we have betrayed His trust, we are reminded that He doesn't give up on us.

As our Loving Teacher and Friend, He encourages the trustworthy student to remain dependable and the untrustworthy student to develop honorable characteristics.

"Don't act thoughtlessly, but try to find out and do whatever the Lord wants you to do." (Ephesians 5:17, Living Bible)

Where To Stop And Rest

The Sunday afternoon was rainy. I was experiencing a case of what some folks call the "Mulley-grubs." Others might label the condition as being "down in the dumps." Whatever the diagnosis, the symptoms of self-pity were evident. That, as has been discovered by many, cannot be overcome with medication.

Returning from an errand, I stopped by for a brief visit with two special friends. The timing was just right to catch their son and his family before they left for home.

After a few minutes of getting acquainted with those two precious grandsons I had heard so much about, a treasured friendship developed. While young brother stood quietly by, the four-year-old demonstrated his musical talent. Picking up a guitar, the youngster strummed his own tune and began singing, "You are my sunshine, my only sunshine . . ."

Finishing his solo, he looked up at his dad and suggested, "Let's do a duet."

It seemed as if Psalms 139:3 was written especially for the occasion. *"You chart the path ahead of me, and tell me where to stop and rest."* (Living Bible)

Needless to say, my "Mulley-grubs" disappeared and the sun came shining through the rain!

Young Friends Fill Deficiency

Hiring a professional domestic engineer would be a waste of God's money, even if I felt I could afford it. God has blessed me with good health. My time is not so filled that I cannot attend to household chores. But, I do have a slight "Vitamin A" deficiency -- that's "A" for ambition!

So occasionally, when the urge strikes to give the house a thorough going over, I will enlist the services of some of my young friends who are willing to lend a helping hand. I have found these young ladies to be cheerful and enthusiastic as they perform their duties. Whatever the assignment, they take pride in doing a good job and are more concerned over helping than of earning money. It is mighty nice to have such young friends who enjoy helping and whose parents are willing for them to help.

My young helpers usually feel they have contributed very little, but they have done what a professional domestic engineer could not do. They have given me a boost and helped turn the task at hand into a pleasant experience. A professional engineer would have been paid to do for me what I should do for myself.

"And whatsoever ye do, do heartily as to the Lord." (Colossians 3:23)

Little Guy Accepts Why

"Thou shalt therefore obey the voice of the Lord thy God and do His commandments." (Deuteronomy 27:10)

"Little Guy" was one of the special youngsters who occasionally visited with my husband and me. Having an inquisitive mind, the little fellow usually asked one question after another. Like most three-year-olds, one of his biggest questions was, "Why?"

A simple explanation usually satisfied his mind. Sometimes even a "Because I said so!" proved acceptable.

One afternoon, while Little Guy was with us, we had relatives to come for a visit. Since it was nap-time for the youngster, he was bedded-down and told I wasn't going to talk with him anymore for a while. Naturally, he wanted to know "Why?"

"Because," he was told, "I've been talking with you all afternoon and I want to talk with Aunt Betty now."

Without giving any argument, the little fellow agreed, "O.K." Then, turning over, he soon drifted off to sleep.

Little Guy's acceptance of and obedience to the answer he received was commendable. "How many times have God's children questioned His instructions?", I wondered. We would do well to remember the little fellow's response to the answer he was given when he questioned, "Why?" God's answers are not always understood but should always be accepted.

When He instructs us as to what He would have us do, we should not put up an argument. We should willingly reply . . . "O.K.!"

Bouquet Conveys Love

"Full of honor and majesty is His work, and His righteousness endures forever." (Psalms 111:3, RSV)

The bouquet that sat on my window sill was a small one. The flowers were not cultivated by man, nor were they arranged by a florist. Fragrance from the several sprigs of wild honeysuckle sweetened the air. Other dainty blossoms from God's garden of nature added color to the arrangement.

Gathered by two of my young friends during an afternoon stroll with their parents, the "bouquet of love" was left for me while I was away from home.

Placing the flowers in a container of water, I was touched by the beauty of the blossoms and the thoughtfulness of my two young friends.

Could anything be more beautiful than a "bouquet of love" gathered from God's garden of nature by the hands of a child?

Good Little Bad Boy

"I'm bad . . . I'm bad!" The child's voice echoed throughout a grocery store. Trailing the sound of the voice, I discovered a little fellow, not more than two-years-old, being wheeled around in a shopping cart. The adult pushing the cart smiled with approval as the youngster continued the repetitious chant.

Thinking it might at least influence the adult, I made an effort to change the little fellow's tune. "Oh, you don't look like a bad boy to me," I said. "I'll bet you are a good boy."

Without delay, the child responded, "I'm bad . . . I'm bad!" Wheeling the cart on down the aisle, the smiling adult confirmed, "Yes, you ARE a bad boy!"

Long after I left the grocery store, the sound of that little voice chiming, "I'm bad . . . I'm bad!" lingered in my mind.

Some parents tease their children, telling them they are bad and it has no ill effect. But this child was so insistent as he voiced the words he had been taught to repeat, I believe he was convinced. Maybe not. Maybe he will learn differently when he learns to distinguish between "being bad" and "being good."

I am reminded of a young lady who became an instant mother to a two-year-old when she and his dad were married. The new mother was concerned that the child sometimes made the statement, "I'm a bad boy."

"I really don't know where he got the idea," said the new mother, "But he really believes it."

Guiding him toward overcoming his negative attitude, the mother talked with the youngster, assuring him that he is a "good boy."

"If you lead a child to believe he is bad, you can expect him to be bad," she said, "because children will be what they think you want them to be."

How fortunate is the child who receives guidance towards developing self-esteem.

"For as he thinketh in his heart, so is he." (Proverbs 23:7a)

Search For Meaningful Life

Nearing his second birthday, a great-nephew of mine spent an afternoon with his "Auntie Een." Deciding to investigate my kitchen, the youngster began opening and closing all the drawers. After checking each drawer, he ventured to the cabinet doors. Peeking behind the doors, finding nothing of special interest, he went from one to another.

Finally, a discovery was made. Opening a door that revealed something more than the ordinary, the little fellow's eyes lit up and he excitedly exclaimed, "Wow!" He looked no further.

The discovery made by the youngster and his reactions illustrates what can be expected in the search for a meaningful life. We need only to open the right door. The door which reveals something more than the ordinary. The one that fills us with excitement. When that door is opened, there is no reason or desire to search any further.

"And ye shall seek me, and find me, when ye shall search for me with all your heart." (Jeremiah 29:13)

Is It Important?

Desiring to speak out "just one more time," a talkative student held her hand high. Having grown weary of unnecessary interruptions, this substitute teacher chose to disregard the silent plea.

Finally, the persistent student was recognized along with the caution, "If it's important, let us hear it. If not, I would appreciate no further interruptions."

Hesitating for a moment, the young lady sweetly replied, "It's important to me." Nothing more of the incident is recalled, but value is found in the student's sincere response.

"It's important to me" . . . Is this not our usual purpose for turning to God? Jesus explained to His disciples that they should always pray and not give up. The parable recorded in Luke 18:1-8 still holds true.

God does not keep us waiting with hands raised when we long to be recognized. Neither does He caution us not to interrupt Him with unimportant matters. Whatever is important to us is important to God because He loves us and we are important to Him!

Reaching For The Forbidden

Exploring the surroundings of a home where his family was visiting, a toddler reached out for a forbidden object. Knowing very well what to expect from his parents, he eased his hand toward the object while casting a glance in their direction. The temptation being too great to resist, the youngster cautiously picked up the object. He then suffered the consequences of disrespecting the teachings of his parents.

The little fellow has such a keen awareness of what to expect that sometimes when reaching for the forbidden with one hand, he holds the other out to be spanked.

Now isn't that a typical illustration of how we, as children of God sometimes conduct ourselves? We have learned to distinguish between the permissible and the forbidden things of life. Yet, when faced with temptation, our personal wants are subject to rule our decisions. Knowing we are inviting trouble, we reach for the forbidden with one hand while holding the other out for God to spank.

There is nothing new about this. It has been going on since Adam and Eve were overcome with temptation stemming from wanting that which was forbidden.

"The woman saw the trees as being good for food, delightful to the eye and a tree desirable to render one wise, so she took of its fruit." (Genesis 3:6, Modern)

Each Will Receive Reward

A youth invested a great deal of time and effort into preparing for an important event. When the date of the event arrived, a hopeful contestant gathered with other hopefuls to await the announcement. Meeting the challenge with a positive outlook, the youth anticipated being named winner of the competition.

Each judge, fulfilling responsibilities according to his or her knowledge and abilities, evaluated all aspects involved in making a decision. Much to his disappointment, someone else was named winner. It was quite a let-down for the youth when he was advised by one judge that his work could have been better.

The young person's experience is one we can all relate to. Having earnestly tried, he was expectant of being recognized as the best in his category. Yet, even his best was not good enough when compared with another by the judge.

That's competition! Some excel in one thing - some another. Some win - some lose. Not everyone can claim the title of champion. Whatever the undertaking, when using our God given talents in an acceptable manner, we will not be disappointed over someone else being awarded that which we anticipated.

When we stand before our Judge, we will not be in competition with a group of contestants. Judged by our own merits, we can expect to hear Him say, *"Well done, thou good and faithful servant."* (Matthew 25:21a)

And, in my imagination, I hear these words compassionately added, *"Receive ye your crown..."*

Prayer Of Mind And Heart

My personal letter to President Ronald Reagan in 1984, and letters from millions of other supporters, upholding prayer in public schools were not sufficient in re-establishing the practice we believe could be beneficial to students and teachers. So, prayer in public schools, as determined by authorized lawmakers, is prohibited. Open prayer, that is. Prayer, however, which can be eliminated from classroom procedure, cannot be prohibited from the mind and heart.

This recognized fact was unintentionally illustrated by a young student who stood before his class to lead the pledge of allegiance to the flag of our country. Calling his classmates to order for the patriotic ritual, the student began . . . "Our Father . . ." As might be expected, there were some snickers and giggles throughout the classroom. Laughter phased out and order was restored as the good-natured lad promptly began the pledge of allegiance.

The amusing incident created a lot of smiley faces. And, the day of this substitute teacher was most definitely made brighter as a result of the existence of "Our Father" having been openly acknowledged.

"When we draw near to God, He draws near to us." (Reference to James 4:8)

Love Made Difference

He was of another nationality and could speak no English when he enrolled in an elementary school in his new homeland - America. The center of attention, the new student was surrounded by boys and girls his own age who wanted to help him adjust to his new environment. They were anxious to help him learn to speak, to read, to write as other Americans.

Teachers worked with the new student, helping him to feel secure. Every sign of progress was recognized. He was praised by his classmates and teachers as he steadily learned to communicate. Only kindness was shown the lad.

Soon he was smiling and saying "Hi!" to his new friends. Soon he was saying words that could be interpreted. Soon he was putting words together to form short sentences. Soon he was reading aloud in class.

It must have been a difficult time to change to a completely new lifestyle, but nurtured in love and responding with love, the new student felt accepted.

"As God's chosen, set apart and enjoying His love, clothe yourselves with tenderness of heart, kindliness, humility, gentleness, patient endurance." (Colossians 3:12, Modern)

Look For An Excuse To Praise

"Do not withhold good from those to whom it is due when it is in your power to do it." (Proverbs 3:27)

When Doug, my first grandson was learning to climb into his high chair, his father stood by cheering him on toward his goal. After much effort the toddler reached the top, sat down and looked to his father for approval. My son proudly hugged his child and showered him with praise for his new accomplishment.

Within a matter of minutes, Doug was climbing up and down with ease, each time turning with outstretched arms to receive the hugs and praises of his father.

We each have a deep need to be recognized and appreciated.

King Solomon, in his wisdom, recognized that a mark of a true leader is the ability to give "good" when it is due. This includes praise. We can feel good about life and earn respect from those around us by following the advice of King Solomon. Just look for an excuse to praise someone.

It is amazing to see how often the opportunity arises to give praise to those to whom it is due.

Spread Love Along Life's Highway

She wanted to give her little visitor something as he left her home. He was dressed for a trip to town, so the sticky candy and the juicy plum were both ruled out. Walking out the door with the child, the lady plucked a red geranium blossom and handed it to him.

Pleased over his flower, the little fellow kept it close at hand. When he returned home, he filled a cup with dirt, planted his flower and gave it to his mother. Later, when "Show and Tell" time rolled around at his school, the child proudly displayed his red geranium. Although the blossom was beginning to wilt, there was promise of the plant taking on new life through the sprouting of roots. The amount of love generated through the one geranium blossom and a young child is amazing.

First, was the love shown by the giver, who thought her gift was small. But, think of the lives it touched. Love, received by the child, was passed on to his mother, then to friends at school. With the possibility of growing into a fruitful plant bearing more blossoms, the geranium's love will reach even further.

Like the one red geranium blossom and one small child, you and I can spread love along life's pathway by touching as many lives as possible.

"May the Lord make (our) love grow and overflow to each other and to everyone else." (I Thessalonians 3:12a, Living Bible)

Bubble Gum Giver

The little girl, probably not more than three-years-old, was engaged in play when she suddenly blurted out, "I've got some bubblegum at home . . . I'm going to get me some. I'll be right back."

Dashing away, the child headed home for her bubblegum. After a few minutes, she returned, chewing away on her gum. Rejoining her friends, the little girl cheerfully announced, "Here's some for you . . . and you . . . and you." Handing out the gum, the child demonstrated scriptural sharing.

Learning at an early age to share something as unimportant as bubblegum is instilling the spirit of sharing more needful things with others as she matures physically and spiritually. Her generosity with the bubblegum today will be reflected in her generosity with toys, food, clothing, money, and giving of self when she has reached adulthood.

The child was not compelled to bring back bubblegum for the others, but that was part of her plan. She ungrudgingly thought beyond herself.

"Let each one give as he has planned in his heart, neither grudgingly nor by compulsion for God loves a happy giver." (II Corinthians 9:7, Modern)

Smiles Reveal Gladness From Within

My youngest grandson, Ben, was no more than four-months-old when he was carried to a Nursing Home to visit his great-grandmother. The moment Ben entered the door, gloomy expressions of residents changed to radiance.

Those dear people, so many of them lonely, were delighted over the appearance of a baby. Most of the residents smiled, talked to Ben, and had to reach out and touch his small hands.

Just as delighted over all the attention he was receiving, Ben flashed broad smiles back to each of his admirers. So young and so innocent, there was nothing pretentious about the little fellow's reaction. His smiles, his cooing and his wrapping those tiny fingers around fingers of aging hands, were all spontaneous reactions.

The certified legal value of a smile is estimated to be $20,000! But, can the worth of a smile be actually determined by the dollar mark? A genuine smile is an unspoken way of saying, *"Thou hast put gladness in my heart."* (Psalms 4:7)

Smiles exchanged in the Nursing Home on Ben's visit most definitely reflected gladness from within hearts.

Looking Out For Another

A Brownie Girl Scout and another young girl canvassed the neighborhood, drumming up cookie sales. This prospective customer asked that they call back later. Leaving my home, the Brownie's friend called out, "Now, don't buy from anybody else, remember to buy from her."

The afternoon of their return, the two-some was accompanied by another Brownie Girl Scout and a young lad. Each Brownie had in hand a partially-filled cookie order form. All four youngsters were eager to boost their sales, competing for prizes to be awarded according to the number of sales. The Brownie who had previously been by was the first to speak, but not for personal gain.

Calling attention to her almost-filled order form and to the other Brownie's form with only a few orders listed, the young saleslady said: "Order from her 'cause I've got more than she's got." Such a sweet and unselfish attitude!

She was taking orders for cookies, but the little Brownie Girl Scout innocently dished out a hearty serving of food for thought. Both girls made a sale, leaving behind an impressive example of Philippians 2:4: *"Neither must each be looking out for his own interests but also for those of others."*

Singing Stops Sobbing

All was quite in the stillness of the night when suddenly the household was awakened by a loud thud, followed by cries of an alarmed child. Falling to the floor from his bed, the upset youngster cried uncontrollably. Efforts to comfort the child were made by his mother and father. Nothing calmed the little one until his mother began singing, while holding him in her arms. Almost instantly, the sobbing ceased and the child relaxed.

It was as though a magic spell had been cast over the little fellow as his mother sang the tune, "Jesus Loves Me."

But, we know magic is trickery. And, we know there is no trickery involved where the love of Jesus is concerned. Through the mother's lulling voice, reassuring her child of Jesus' love, came the same calmness as the calm that swept across the troubled waters when Jesus rebuked the raging storm, and said to the sea: *"Peace, be still."* (Mark 4:39)

Peace comes when Jesus speaks. He can "calm the troubled waters of the soul."

Something New

Selected by my grandson, Doug, from a stack of children's story books for "Grandma" to read aloud, was one about a little girl who wanted to add variety to her life. Thinking of all the fun things she would like to do, she began making plans for each day of the week.

The schedule was a busy one filled with lots of exciting events. On Monday, the little girl went to the zoo. Tuesday, she visited a farm, and Wednesday was spent at the seashore. Thursday was a day at the amusement park. Friday was spent observing fish in a gigantic aquarium. On Saturday, the circus was the big attraction.

The week's schedule was completed except for Sunday, which had been reserved for "something new." By the time Sunday rolled around, the little girl was so exhausted from having had so much fun during the week that all she wanted to do was stay at home and take it easy.

And so, the little girl's story had an all too familiar ending, with no place in her busy week for Sunday School and worship services. Perhaps this would have been "something new" for the child, as it would be for many people in real life.

That "something new", when made a regular part of scheduled activities, is instrumental in finding an exciting way of life, and gives one cause to say: *"I was glad when they said unto me, Let us go into the House of the Lord."* (Psalms 122:1)

Closer Look Helps Vision

"Open my eyes to see wonderful things in Your Word." (Psalms 119:18, Living Bible)

In his book, *"Kids Say The Darndest Things",* Art Linkletter shares amusing experiences from his interviews with youngsters.

The book is appropriately titled. Children do, indeed, often come out with innocent remarks that are amusing. But, they are also capable of making "common sense" remarks as well.

Such was the case of a seven-year-old when her mother's eyeglasses were broken. Without glasses the mother had double-vision. Said the seven-year-old, "Mother, maybe God wants you to take a closer look at things." Giving thought to her young daughter's comment, the mother realized a closer look at things would be required while she was without glasses. By carefully taking a closer look, the mother was able to perform her duties with ease.

"Things look a little blurry, but I've learned which of the two visions is the real thing, and that's the one I keep my attention focused on," she said. "It's not so bad after all."

Problems sometimes result from looking too far ahead, even for those whose physical vision is not impaired.

It's worth thinking about: When life becomes blurry and we are seeing double, it stands to reason that God wants us to take a closer look, distinguish between the existing and non-existing images, and focus our attention on that which is real.

Grabbing For Cookies

A youngster was offered a cookie. Reaching out with one hand, the cookie was received. But, the one cookie only made the youngster want more. With its childlike nature, the little one reached out with the other hand for another cookie.

What might seem to be greediness is merely typical. That's just the way children are. If they had six hands, all six would reach out for cookies. This human characteristic, instilled at birth, seems to carry over into adulthood. We want - we receive - we want more.

Even in our relationship with God, we have a tendency not to be completely satisfied. When we have received something in one hand, we reach out with the other, expecting it to be filled. God, who provides our needs and desires, is a generous God. He gives, and gives, and gives. He gives those daily blessings that come so automatically that we take them for granted.

He gives those material things that we could easily do without when we reach for a "cookie" in each hand. And, to those who will receive, God fills our lives with spiritual blessings that make the "cookies" we grab for become insignificant.

"I will give you a new heart - I will give you new and right desires - and put a new spirit within you. I will take out your stony hearts of sin and give you new hearts of love." (Ezekiel 36:26, Living Bible)

True Friend's Door Remains Open

"Anxiety in a man's heart weighs him down, but a good word makes him glad." (Proverbs 12:25, RSV)

Two children played happily together in the yard until the thing that often happens between children at play happened. A disagreement between the two sent one child homeward bound. The other child trailed closely behind. Both children, equally determined to have the last word, quarreled each step of the way.

The child in the lead "closed the door" on the argument when she stepped inside her home and abruptly slammed the door in the face of her playmate. Turning away in anger, the rejected child muttered to herself as she made her way home. The two were no longer friends. They were never going to play together again. The broken friendship lasted as long as most broken friendships between children last. The two were soon back at play as if nothing ever happened.

Whatever the problem, the children had resolved their differences. The wounds had healed. Their friendship was renewed.

It is unfortunate that friendships are sometimes wounded, but the beauty of true friendships is that they are never permanently dissolved. Time heals all wounds where love holds priority over anger. Doors are closed on arguments, but never on true friendships.

Identity Should Be No Problem

"Cute." That was my first impression of the shirt worn by the little toddler. Then it struck me as to how unnecessary the lettering, "T-Shirt, T-Shirt, T-Shirt," stretched across the front of the shirt was. Anybody could look at the garment and recognize it as being a T-Shirt. Of course, the lettering was not intended for identification. It was meant to be cute, and cute it was. But, the cute T-Shirt gave me something to think about.

I thought about the number of times we have heard someone ask, "Is he a Christian?", or "Are you a Christian?" And, I thought about the number of times we have heard the declaration made, "He is a fine Christian man." "She is a wonderful Christian woman," or "I am proud to be a Christian."

It is natural for Christians to be concerned over the spiritual welfare of others, and Christians have every reason to be proud of their heritage. But, just as the garment could be identified without the lettering, "T-Shirt, T-Shirt, T-Shirt," there should be no question about the identity of a Christian.

"If we live, we live to the Lord and if we die, we die to the Lord. So then, whether we live or we die, we belong to the Lord." (Romans 14:8, Amplified Bible)

Rusty Heels Insignificant

Seldom do I step into a steaming shower without remembering a child who was the target of criticism for having "rusty heels."

The child in mention was a barefooted country lad. He lived and worked on a farm. Drinking water, bath water, and water for any other purpose had to be drawn from a well, carried into the house by buckets-full, and heated on a wood burning stove. In some cases, tubs of water were heated outside by warm rays from the sunshine. Most likely the child did not have access to a bathtub. If he did, there was no time to soak in warm suds that did not stay warm for long.

Facing reality, we know there is no justification for the child's rusty heels, even under his penalized circumstances. But, neither was there any justification in the criticism heaped upon the lad who worked hard, wore clean clothes and was of good character. It would have been just as easy to lavish the lad with praise for his commendable qualities. Had the lad been looked upon for his good qualities, the rusty heels would have been insignificant.

It is the hearts of people, not their heels, that should be focused upon.

"He that hath clean hands, and a pure heart; who hath not lifted up his soul unto vanity, nor sworn deceitfully; He shall receive the blessings from the Lord, and righteousness from the God of His salvation." (Psalms 24:4-5)

Lot To Be Learned From Children

Little ones! Aren't they precious and can't we learn a lot from them?

My youngest grandson has latched on to a number of adult friends who have won his affection simply through love. He responds rather enthusiastically at the mention of their names and gets highly excited when he sees them. The little fellow has not been brain-washed to display the love that began at a tender age and will go with him through life. No one has to point out his special friends. He can spot them in a crowd. No one has to give him a nudge, or prompt him to call out their names or pass out hugs. His reactions are natural, and of his own accord.

My grandson is no different in this respect from other youngsters who know the security of being loved and giving love in return. Little ones who know, and so readily welcome this type of love have something in common with children of God in their relationship to Jesus Christ. It does not take brain-washing for a relationship with Jesus Christ to be cultivated. No one has to give the child of God a nudge or call out His name or to reach out to Him with loving hearts.

The reactions of a child of God to the Greatest Friend anyone could ever have comes naturally, without any prompting from anyone. Just to catch a glimpse of Him, or merely hear the mention of His name, creates excitement and enthusiasm.

"Blessed be His glorious name forever: and let the whole earth be filled with His glory." (Psalms 72:19)

No Bargains Or Threats

The three-year-old child sat around the dining table with her family. While others ate of the meal, the little girl picked over her food, finding reasons not to eat.

"You must eat your dinner if you want dessert," she was calmly promised by her mother. Still, the child was not enthused over eating her dinner. The food was "too hot." It burned her throat. She was "too full."

Everyone else finished their meal. The table was cleared, including the unfinished meal left by the child who was not hungry. Ice cream was dipped and served along with cookies made by "Granny." An excited little girl returned to the table, climbed upon her booster seat and waited wistfully for ice cream and cookies. She was calmly asked one question by her mother, "Are you hungry enough to eat your dinner now?"

Without a moment's hesitation, the child replied, "Yes!"

There was no bargaining. No threats were made. She was not overly coaxed. The child was simply enticed to eat her meal by a mother who keeps her promises! The little girl soon cleaned her dish, knowing the mother would come through with the ice cream and cake.

Just as the mother was true to her promise, God is true to the promises he makes to His children.

"There hath not failed one word of all His good promises." (I Kings 8:56b)

Now, That's Nice!

"What is the nicest thing that has ever happened to you?"

Answers to that question by a group of youngsters are varied. "Getting a horse for my birthday," said one. "Moving into a big house," said another. Family gatherings, special gifts on special occasions, going on trips, getting to do "fun things," and spending time with friends. These were among the things that registered in the minds of the young boys and girls as the nicest things they had ever experienced.

Several of the youngsters felt their lives were void of anything nice. "Life," as described these, is "dull and boring." One with an apparently brighter outlook said, "Being born is the nicest thing that has ever happened to me."

"The nicest thing that ever happened to me was one night at church when I walked up and joined the church and on the following Sunday, I got baptized! Now that's nice!", exclaimed a young lady who had turned her life over to God.

Life is not meant to be "dull and boring," and it need not be. Life, itself, should be one of the nicest things that has ever happened to anyone. Beyond that, the experience of being "born again" should head up the list. For (then) you have a new life. It was not passed on to you from your parents, for the life they gave you will fade away. This new one will last forever, for it comes from Christ, God's ever-living message to men." (Reference: I Peter 1:23, Living Bible)

Not Perfect, Just Forgiven!

A young person told of seeing a Sunday School teacher enter a package store during a holiday season. Continuing to watch, the quiet observer related seeing the teacher leave with a bottle-shaped package.

The teacher, believed to be an abstainer, could have made the purchase for cooking purposes. Regardless of how innocent the adult in question was, the reflection was damaging to the younger individual who could not understand what appeared to be double standards.

Puzzled over the situation, the youth not only lost confidence in the teacher, but confidence in the church was also destroyed for the time.

How often might we have been seen conducting ourselves in such a way that would cause our Christianity to be questioned.

In a sense, Christians are comparable to tightrope walkers. Whether walking on a rope extended high into the air or with our feet on the ground, the requirements are the same. If we are to maintain steady balance, we must be surefooted.

Traveling through Hern, Texas, I read these words from a church bulletin board: "As Christians, We're Not Perfect, Just Forgiven."

Christians are tightrope walkers. We lose our balance - we slip - we fall - God in His loving mercy is there to catch us - lift us up - help us on our feet again.

We, like David, can say: *"I will extol thee, O Lord, because Thou hast lifted me, and hast not let my enemies rejoice over me."* (Psalms 30:1)

Let us pray that observers will recognize the reality of the slogan posted on that church bulletin board as we strive towards not leading anyone astray.

Qualities Developed Through Lifestyles

Striving to discourage frequent use of unkind words, I asked a class of fifth graders to list words they did not like to hear. The motive, of course, was to create an awareness of considerate language.

This compiled list, seemingly endless, revealed the common words "shut-up" as being the number one unkind phrase. Also topping the list were expressions made famous by characters of certain television programs.

Results of the experiment were favorable at the time, as students began to catch and correct their own unkind words.

It is a known fact however, that experiments do not always produce lasting value. Our qualities - good or bad - are developed through the lifestyle we choose.

This experiment could also be a helpful means of encouraging more consideration among those within the family unit. Slogan: "If you don't want to hear it, don't say it!"

A scriptural slogan, applicable to our day-to-day speech could be taken from Colossians 4:6: *"Let your conversation be gracious as well as sensible."* (Living Bible)

Each One Capable

"If you are not a straight 'A' student, why aren't you?", a class of students was directly asked. The motive was to suggest devoting more time to more important things and less time to the lesser of importance. There is no denying this as the solution for many students who settle for lower grades than they are capable of making.

This however, is not always the case. There are some students who really work for whatever grades they achieve and rate a "pat on the back." To suggest their failure of being "straight A" students due to lack of interest, is inconsiderate.

Learning comes easier to some than to others. Some want to learn, others lack the desire. Some try, others put forth no effort whatsoever. Some believe in themselves, others lack self-confidence. No matter what the goal, making the best of one's education is important.

Needless to say it didn't take 42 years of marriage and a few less years of motherhood for my eyes to be opened to the necessity of those subjects that seemed so unnecessary in my younger days.

What should have been better learned could be useful in so many ordinary ways. For examples: balancing the checkbook, helping children with homework, carrying on an intelligent conversation or writing a simple column and reading road maps while hubby drives . . . he wishes I could!

Everyone has capabilities. Whatever is done should be done with pride and to the best of one's abilities. To be content with anything less is an injustice to self and to God.

To my young friends who are doing their best, this bit of encouragement is offered: "Keep up the good work!" Those who are permitting opportunities to slip by will one day look back with regrets, but those lost moments cannot be reclaimed.

Remember this advice recorded in Proverbs 1:5: *"The wise man also may hear and increase in learning, and the man of understanding acquire skill."* (RSV)

Wiggling Clear Of God's Hand

A young man gently placed his hand over a cricket . . . the cricket hopped from beneath the hollow of his hand. Again the young man placed his hand over the cricket . . . again the cricket jumped from beneath the shelter.

Succeeding in his attempt to rescue the cricket from danger, the young man carried the little creature to a safe location and released it.

The incident held a true-to-life illustration. God sees us in dangerous situations. He reaches out to rescue us. Not always aware of our predicament, we sometimes wiggle our way clear of His hand. He does not snatch us up, but lovingly He reaches out again and again, ready to set us free.

If we will humble ourselves under the mighty hand of God, in His good time He will lift us up.

"Let Him have all your worries and cares, for He is always thinking about you and watching everything that concerns you." (I Peter 5:6-7, Living Bible)

'Cause His Hand Is Bigger Than Mine!

I like the little anecdote that has been told of a young lad who accompanied his mother to the grocery store. Entering the store, the youngster was greeted by a grocer who invited the lad to help himself to a handful of freshly harvested cherries. Not being over-anxious to "dig" into the basket of delicious fruit, the hesitant lad stood quietly beside his mother.

"Don't you like cherries?", the grocer asked. "Yes," the lad replied.

Later, the puzzled mother asked the son why he had not taken the cherries when the offer was first made. "'Cause his hand is bigger than mine," the lad truthfully admitted.

A touch of humor in the incident generates a smile, or perhaps a chuckle as the scene is envisioned. But, there's another side to the story. The lad could have helped himself and gone his merry way with a small handful of cherries. His motive could be thought of as greed. Or, perhaps he was motivated by wisdom and patience. The lad was wise enough to realize the grocer would give him more than he could have gotten on his own. He was patient and trusting enough to wait for a more generous serving from the hand of the grocer.

So it is as we receive gifts from God. We can grab a little handful for ourselves and be on our way. Or, we can patiently wait, trusting God for the generous servings He will give directly.

"The Lord is good to those who wait for Him." (Lamentations 3:25) If we give Him time, He will surely fulfill our every need.

His mighty hand is so much bigger than ours!

Stay Spiritually Connected

The intelligence of young people never ceases to amaze me. A thirteen-year-old boy stopped by our house one afternoon. In one hand the boy carried a small, out-of-order tape player. In the other hand he held a short wire.

To restore performance to the tape player, the wire had to be properly attached to the points of contact. There were a lot of places the wire could have been connected, but only one place that would be effective.

The thirteen-year-old knew exactly where the wire belonged. I was captivated by the boy as he demonstrated his patience and ability to make the delicate repair. Within a matter of minutes the wire was replaced - connection made - service restored. It wasn't nearly as complicated as it appeared to be.

We, too, have a point of contact. When our spiritual connection is broken it puts the Christian out of order. The Christian knows exactly what needs to be done and how to go about it in order to restore effective performance. It's not the least bit complicated.

"Draw nigh to God, and He will draw nigh to you." (James 4:8)

Premature 'A-Men' Is Like Putting Cart Before Horse

Reaching the end of his regular table grace, the little fellow paused. Prompting him to conclude the prayer, his mother said, "A-Men."

"Don't say 'A-Men'," the youngster stated in a very definitive tone of voice. He then proceeded to give thanks for his parents, grandparents, the sun, the moon, the stars, flowers, birds and trees.

After thanking God for everything that entered his young mind, he was ready for the "A-Men." It had not troubled the little fellow in the least that the food was getting cold or that others were anxious to eat. He had a thankful heart and wanted to take time to voice his praise to God.

In all probability, the youngster will learn to keep his mealtime prayer of thanksgiving brief. He, too, will reach the age that his mind will be focused more on the good food in front of him than on all the other gifts that flow freely from God. But, hopefully, he will not outgrow his appreciation of family, nature, and the necessities and luxuries of life.

In this hurried life, not everyone takes time to say, "Thank You," to God. Let us learn to give thanks without getting in such a big hurry to say, "A-Men."

"O, give thanks to the Lord for He is good; for His steadfast love endures forever!" (I Chronicles 16:34, RSV)

Come As A Little Child Unto The Lord

"You know he can't walk by himself," said the little girl of her toddling baby brother. "He must have someone who loves him to hold his hand and walk beside him."

As I sat on the park bench and watched the two children walk across the green grass, the younger was hesitant, stumbly, slow, looking upwards with confidence into the encouraging, smiling face of his "big" sister.

I thought of the story of Moses and the nation of Israel. Moses knew that the people needed to be taught to walk by the Word of God and it was up to him to teach them.

So many times, people can't live happy and abundant lives without someone to walk and talk with them, to encourage and lead the way. Perhaps this is what the scripture - Psalms 23:4 - is saying: *"Yea, though I walk through the valley of the shadow of death, I will fear no evil, for Thou art with me."*

We need to respond to God's love and mercy by glorifying Him with living each day in a righteous way.

There are times when we forget and feel bewildered, as the little boy mentioned above, as we stumble down the pathway of life. We forget to walk in the ways pleasing to Jesus. We know that God's Holy Spirit has been given to us to assist in this walk of life.

We must come as a little child unto the Lord and realize the truth of the Word which says in Psalms 84:11, *"No good thing will He withhold from them that walk uprightly."*

(Written and contributed by my good friend, **Sarah Conley***, during her battle with cancer. She fought a courageous fight!)*

Chapter Two

Selected From Files

Letting Go Of Hurt

Children are so precious - so sweet - so innocent. They are so loving and so forgiving. This was evidenced in the "flash of a moment" when Casey visited with her Aunt Earline and Uncle Robert several years ago.

Casey was at the wheel of the old dune buggy that stands in our yard. The old vehicle, stripped of its engine and other parts to make it go, brings much enjoyment to young children.

In her sharp little mind, Casey was traveling down the road. Suddenly, she came to a screeching halt, jumped from the dune buggy and said, "I know what I can do, this rock can be what I got for you."

No sooner had Casey picked up the rock, "Aunt Earline" abruptly ordered her to put that rock down and leave those rocks alone. After studying the rocks outlining a flower bed, this small one had just been placed where it seemed to belong. Now, it had been disrupted and even after numerous attempts, the rocks could not be rearranged to look the same. Instructions were repeated to Casey that she was never to mess with my rocks.

Oh, sure, I was a little tired from working with the rocks, but that did not justify my being so harsh with Casey. It would have been just as easy to say, "Hey, that's a good idea. You can give me the rock, but when we get through playing, let's put the rock back where it was." Casey would have been fine with that.

Bless her sweet little heart, Casey put the rock down and was unhappy momentarily. She hopped back into the dune buggy and continued her make believe journey. The smile returned to her face and she was back to her happy little self as if nothing had ever happened.

Chances are she has forgotten the unpleasant situation by now, but Little Casey demonstrated a lesson that we all should practice. Naturally, she was wounded by the harshness of Aunt Earline, but she didn't allow the wound to get in the way of love. Not only did she enjoy the remainder of her stay, but when time arrived for her to go home, she wanted to stay longer.

The memory of the incident still haunts me when I think of how unkind I was to a little child . . . one so sweet and innocent.

It blesses my heart that Casey, as most children, can let go of misunderstandings and go on loving. The spirit of Christ dwells within.

"For You, Lord, are good, and ready to forgive..."
(Psalms 86:5a)

Not Enough Good Said

"If there is anything worthy of praise, think about these things." (Philippians 4:8)

Enough good is not said about our young people today. Society seems to have a tendency to judge all by those spotlighted for their wrongful ways. Fortunately, not all fall into the wayward category.

Visions that rapidly flash through my mind instantly include those wonderful young people found in church on Sunday who reflect the teachings of home and church in their daily living.

Some unchurched young people are also envisioned as well mannered and well behaved youths who are a credit to society.

Some gain deserved recognition for outstanding accomplishments, still there are other youths who go unnoticed, or are seemingly taken for granted.

My rapid vision of teenagers who demonstrate voluntarily thoughtfulness includes:

- One who drove into the church yard where I happened to be at the time. Bringing his vehicle to a stop, the young man made time to speak a friendly word and share a smile.
- Another young man, driving past my home, and still another who knocked upon my door, made time to stop and speak.
- Young people in my neighborhood, who from time to time, honor my husband and me with a visit. There's nothing out of the ordinary about being asked, "Do you have something I can do?"

These simple encounters with the younger generation are but a few examples, but with visions flashing through my mind, I see a multitude of young people who remind me of what the Boy Jesus must have been like.

I visualize Him as a compassionate lad, who, bringing His donkey to a halt, made time to speak a friendly word to someone when it was least expected.

When judging our young people of today, we would do well to look for "Boy Jesus" characteristics, and speak favorable of those qualities that so often go unnoticed, or are so often taken for granted.

Perfect Pattern Taking Shape

"Behold, how good and how pleasant it is for brethren to dwell together in unity!" (Psalms 133:1)

Students of a physics class were studying magnets. As an experiment, each student was given a sheet of paper and a handful of steel shavings. Sprinkling the shavings over the sheet of paper, the students saw nothing more than a bunch of scattered particles with no particular significance.

Placing the particle filled paper over a magnet, they observed a change as the filings were drawn together in beautiful symmetrical patterns. Each particle seemed to have found its place of belonging.

The scientific experiment illustrates how God's magnetic power can help individuals find their place of belonging, bringing people who "stand alone" together to form a meaningful pattern of life.

Strength is gained from one another when it might seem that life is becoming a state of confusion. Drawn together through the magnetic power of God, we can find, and help others to find, joy where there is sorrow . . . love where there is hate . . . contentment where there is confusion.

We then gain a vision of everything in its proper place making a perfect pattern.

Just Read The Directions

"When all else fails, read the directions." -- Chances are that almost everyone has attempted to undertake something in particular without first reading the directions.

It looks so easy. So, disregarding the step-by-step instructions, an attempt is made to accomplish the task at hand within our own power.

If luck is on our side, it is possible to eventually succeed, but not with the ease that comes from following instructions.

Frustrations that often result from undertaking things on our own are so uncalled for and can be avoided by taking time to read and follow directions. As Christians, it is important that we read and follow directions given in the Bible. God's Word teaches us how to live. It helps us to accept situations that we could not cope with on our own.

Reading and applying directions outlined in the Bible relieves us of unnecessary frustrations that are encountered when we attempt to make it on our own. We cannot count on luck to lead us through life. We must follow God's directions!

"Apply thine heart unto instructions, and thine ears to words of knowledge." (Proverbs 23:12, KJV)

Share The Sunshine Of God's Love

"When a man is gloomy, everything seems to go wrong; when he is cheerful, everything seems right."
(Proverbs 15:15, Living Bible)

An elevator operator in a large business establishment was once asked, "You don't get much sunshine in here, do you?" Quick came his reply, "Only what you bring in!"

Seclusion from the light of day need not deprive us of the warmth of sunshine that comes through sharing God's love with one another. The sun does not always shine, but God's love never stops. It never changes.

We can share the sunshine of God's love everywhere we go, even on cloudy days - even in closed elevators.

Flashing a smile to someone . . . speaking words of kindness . . . doing a small deed . . . these are but a few ways we can brighten up a day that might otherwise be gloomy.

God's love in us helps us give encouragement to others. God's love in us helps put new hope and excitement in every day.

We Break Things, But God Fixes

"People . . . places . . . things . . . of all these, people upset me the most." These words, spoken by a disgusted repairman, reflect somewhat of a negative attitude towards life. Influenced by his day-to-day routine of fixing things, the repairman firmly stated that about 99 percent of his problems were brought on by careless people.

"People who break things that have to be fixed and they expect me to fix them," he said. Continuing to voice a great dislike for mankind, the repairman expressed his preference to be completely disassociated with other people.

Pity the poor fellow. Pity anyone with an attitude of this kind towards his fellow man. Where would we be if God shut people out of His life because of our carelessness and clumsiness? Surely, of all things that stand to disturb God, it must be, "we, the people," that disturbs Him the most.

No one is into fixing things nearly as much as God. In all probability it would delight Him to have less repairs to make, but not likely does He desire to completely disassociate Himself with earthly beings, *"for the Lord taketh pleasure in His people."* (Psalms 149:4a)

Still, God goes on fixing those things brought to Him for repair, and loving the people whose souls He mends.

Chapter Three

Halloween

Door Opened To Treat

Halloween comes and Halloween goes. What good can possibly come from children portraying parts of pretentious characters for several hours as they call on neighbors with shouts of "Trick-or-Treat?" . . . "Trick-or-Treat?"

Make believe is a normal part in the life of the average youngster. In their little minds they know their imaginary roles are only temporary. What does a child remember most from the "Trick-or-Treat" adventure? Momentarily, the most important thing is most likely what or how much was collected.

As the child advances from the "Trick-or-Treat" stage to a more realistic one, he or she will place less emphasis on the contribution and more on the contributor. The child will, in years to come, lovingly remember as friends, those who responded to their little shouts of "Trick-or-Treat."

It will not be the bubblegum, the candy, or other goodies that will be remembered, but the person.

When we are beckoned to the door by our young Halloween visitors, the person who opens the door receives a treat in the form of love. Some homes are bypassed by the "Trick-or-Treaters." But, there is One who is not a fictitious character and not merely an annual visitor who never bypasses anyone. He knocks on the heart's door.

The Living Bible quotes Jesus as saying: *"I have been standing at the door and I am constantly knocking. If anyone hears me calling him and opens the door, I will come in and fellowship with him and he with me."* (Revelation 3:20)

The person who opens the door receives a tremendous treat in the form of tremendous love!

Closely Watched

Halloween, though not the most acceptable of celebrated dates, has its favorable points.

Being cautioned against receiving treats which could be camouflaged tricks, most youngsters do not call upon everyone in the neighborhood.

The little ghosts and goblins and other make believe characters are selective as to which homes will be included in their evening of tours.

They go where they know they will be welcomed and know their treat will not be harmful to them. In many cases, time runs out before visits have been completed.

Regardless of personal feelings towards the tradition, we are fortunate to have relationships of this kind with others, especially the younger generation.

On October 31st, when beckoned to the door and greeted with voices chiming "Trick-or-Treat" . . . "Trick-or-Treat", we are being honored in a special way.

As we respond, care should be taken to do so in such a way that the real treat will be in the contact.

"The Lord gazes down upon mankind from heaven where He lives. He has made their hearts and closely watches everything they do." (Psalms 33:13-15, Living Bible)

Polly Punkin-Head's Purpose

Lots of people at the Farmer's Market had lots of pumpkins to sell. The shouts were continuously, "How about a pumpkin?" I continuously shouted back, "Don't need one!"

Making our way down one lane, my husband and I passed a shed with more pumpkins than we had seen anywhere. "How about a pumpkin?", a young man shouted. "Are you giving them away?", I shouted back. "Yes . . . catch!", the young man replied. Surprisingly, he tossed a tiny pumpkin to me. Surprisingly, I caught it from our slow moving automobile!

The pumpkin was so small, I honestly felt sorry for it. It would have made a cute baby Jack-O-Lantern, but carving on the little thing seemed almost cruel.

Reminded that God does not create things that cannot be used in some way, I wondered what useful purpose such a small pumpkin could possibly have. Not being a creative person, I asked God to help me think of something to do with the tiny pumpkin. Maybe it sounds ridiculous to bother God with such an unimportant matter, but I know He understood because it wasn't long before Polly-Punkin-Head was created.

Facial features of roly-eyes, a petite nose and a broad smile were glued in place. Strands of hair from my haircut (after ten years of growth) were added and Polly wore a dainty crocheted pin-cushion hat. Polly's bottle body was draped with material of appropriate colors for the season.

Standing outside my back door, attracting attention, Polly generated smiles from visitors. She was the center of attraction at a meeting where she held a miniature basket filled with candy.

Later, Polly was invited to serve treats at a meeting in the home of a friend. From there, she spent some time at school along with other Halloween creations.

Polly's purpose was soon fulfilled. If she could have talked, I'm sure she would have said, "Thank You, God, for giving me something to do. It has been lots of fun. And, perhaps she would have added, *"Let my soul live, and it shall praise you."* (Psalms 119:175)

Spooky's First Halloween

Spooky Spider was spinning his web
inside a hollow tree,
When he heard a lot of noises
and wondered what they could be.
He eased himself to a knot hole
and crawled into the space,
Where he could hear what was going on
and see what was taking place.
Spooky was frightened half to death,
he wished he'd stayed inside.
But now he dared not move an inch -
not even to run and hide!
Screaming witches and howling ghosts,
such sights he had never seen,
As the scary creatures surrounded him
on his first Halloween.
When the children spied Spooky standing there,
they said, "Don't be afraid
of the costumes we are wearing
and the noises we have made.
We call this 'Trick or Treating',
we'd like to show you how;
Just get a bag and come along,
join in the fun right now!"
Spooky responded without delay,
the children laughed with glee,
When Spooky said, "Usually, I scare people,
but tonight you surely scared me!"

Of course, we know "Spooky Spider" is not real, and that the boys and girls were not real. In fact, nothing about the little poem is real. The whole thing is just as make believe as "Trick-or-Treating" at Halloween.

But there is one thing we can be sure of: there is nothing make believe about God. His love is very real. It was so great that, *"He gave His only Son, that whoever believed in Him should not perish but have eternal life."* (John 3:16, RSV)

Who's Behind That Mask?

Children look forward to the month of October and the opportunity for an adventure in the land of make believe. Many people look upon Halloween as an unchristian event, but to others the evening is an enjoyable experience.

Responding to the little shouts of "Trick-or-Treat" . . . "Trick-or-Treat", we find all sorts of characters, both favorable and unfavorable.

Knowing the real personality is covered up, we are likely to ask, "Who's behind that mask?" When the mask is removed, we see the bright eyed, smiling face, or face of one who is altogether different from the role being portrayed.

Do we not, at times, find ourselves in similar situations as the youngsters on Halloween? As we consider the possibility, we might ask ourselves, "Who's behind that mask?" We then might discover that we too, have been acting out a role for which we were not created. Temporary satisfaction is replaced with fulfillment when we unmask and reveal our true identity.

"The Lord will perfect that which concerneth me: Thy mercy, O Lord, endureth forever, forsake not the work of thine own hands." (Psalms 138:8)

Letter To Young Friends: October 1982

Dear Boys and Girls:

Each Halloween, as I anxiously await your annual visit, sounds of happiness echo from all directions. The world of make believe is one of fun, and I enjoy pretending right along with you. You do such a good job of making believe that most of the time I do not know who you really are.

But, I cannot fool you because you know who I am, where I live, and expect me to be ready for your visit.

There was a time when I dressed as a witch, but now I stick to a more realistic role. Witches are supposed to ride brooms and fly around in the sky, aren't they? Well, that's what we have always heard, anyway. We know it is not true.

Look up at the sky. What do you see? It doesn't matter if it is Halloween or any other night, you know what is really up there. And, on a clear night, don't the stars and moon shine pretty? We know who put them there too, don't we? Of course . . . God did!

The Bible tells us that God made the world and everything in it. Read about it in Genesis, the first book of the Bible. God is such a good friend. In fact, He is the "goodest" friend we will ever have! You know the best part of it all, too, don't you? God is not make believe. He is real! He doesn't play tricks on us either, and He gives us so many treats we cannot keep count of them!

Have a Happy Halloween, and any time you start pretending, don't forget who you really are. Always remember, too, that God loves you and so do I!

"So faith, hope, love abide, these three, but the greatest of these is love." (I Corinthians 13:13, RSV)

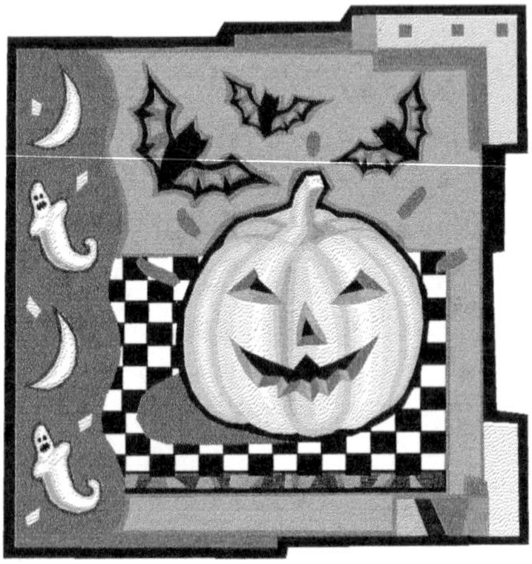

Chapter Four

The Greatest of These Is Love

(Based on writings compiled in 1975)

Examination Of Love

The word "love" is used so loosely in our modern society. It has lost much of its significance. Many think so little of love, they wear it on the seat of their pants where it is either sat upon . . . or kicked around. Others wear it over their heart where real love stems from. We realize the true meaning of love only when we commit our lives to God and live in accordance with His teachings.

Love takes in a large category of other words contained in the dictionary. Among these are:
- Affection
- Compassion
- Concern
- Faith
- Forgiveness
- Gratitude
- Happiness
- Honesty
- Kindness
- Patience
- Respect
- Security
- Sharing
- Sorrow
- Strength
- Suffering
- Understanding
- Unity

Sacrifice is one of the most important words related to love. Jesus sacrificed His life on the cross that we might have life eternal. We say we love God, yet we hesitate to deprive ourselves of time already belonging to Him in order to serve Him. Sacrifice is a *must* in demonstrating true love to God and our fellow man.

When our love for God is genuine, it will be shown

through affection, concern, compassion, kindness, patience, understanding and respect for our fellow man. We cannot say we love and not show that we have faith in those we claim to love. Otherwise, we would be omitting honesty.

Forgiveness is more than just a word. No one is exempt from making mistakes. Love does not permit one to hold grudges or to pass judgment. We must be willing to forgive others in the same manner we expect to be forgiven. Love grows stronger through forgiveness.

To love is to possess a feeling of gratitude for the opportunity of sharing in time of suffering and sorrow as well as times of good fortune. Love gives us strength as security and leads to unity among all.

"Love is happiness -- Happiness in knowing God."
"Happy is that people, whose God is the Lord." (Psalms 144:15b)

Love - In School Traffic

Caught up in the rush
of school traffic
A typical scene
is the display of love
between two people
in the car ahead
While the car is in motion
smiles are exchanged
an arm around a neck
a head resting on the
companion's shoulder.
The traffic light turns red
the driver leans closer
planting a quick kiss
on the cheek.
Mile after mile
the actions are repeated -
the love growing stronger
a binding relationship developing.
Reaching its destination
the car comes to a halt
the two exchange another smile
several other light kisses
and an embrace
Stepping from the car
the driver walks around
opens the door
offers assistance
to the special one
With tenderness and compassion
the passenger
is helped out of the car
Hand in hand
The two stroll from the car
and enter the building

where together they will
laugh, love and learn
How much better
the world would be
with more lovers
of this kind
Because the love described
is that between a young child
and his school teacher mom
on a typical day
of exhibiting
acts of love
in school traffic.

(From "The Greatest Is Love", Earline Ross Cole, 1975)

More Than Coincidence

Serving as a foster home was a rewarding part of the lives of my family, though it was sad to know the children who were "visiting" with us were there due to unfortunate circumstances within their own family unit.

One experience to be considered mere coincidence by many, will linger in my memory for years to come.

Among the 25 children cared for during five short years of service were a three-year-old boy and his baby sister. Our caseworker had set up an appointment for the brother to spend a day with his mother. Since foster parents and natural parents were not permitted to know the identity of each other, arrangements had been made for us to meet our caseworker at a given time. The child was to be left at the office where the mother would pick him up. Reversed arrangements were made for the child's return later in the evening.

Arriving at the office of Family Services, my husband and I discovered the caseworker had not arrived. Seating ourselves in the hall, we began our wait. After 30-45 minutes, the entrance door opened. The young mother, looking to be no more than sixteen or seventeen, appeared. You can believe that was, without a doubt, the happiest little boy in the world!

With excitement in his voice, he called out, "Mama", and his eyes sparkled as he ran to meet her. Giving his mother a big hug, he planted a kiss on her cheek. The affection was returned.

We couldn't have a reunion because of never having met before. But for another 30 minutes we sat together and had ourselves a real "union."

A surprised caseworker reached her office. Realizing she would be late, another worker was expected to fill in for her. The caseworker on call was unaware of our presence. Being unaware of the "set up", we made no effort to look for her.

After meeting the mother, it was impossible for me to be content knowing how much love she and her children were missing from each other.

Finally, the caseworker gave in to my tearful pleas and permitted the mother to visit in our home. This was the beginning of a lasting friendship . . . one that was surely more than "mere coincidence", but was a part of God's plan.

It's true - there were problems in the home, but there was love in the mother's heart. Upon seeing the mother, the child's happiness reflected that . . . "The greatest of these is love."

"Miss Lizzie"

It has been sixty or more years since "Miss Lizzie" lived in the house behind Milner Methodist Church. "Miss Lizzie", an elderly lady, lived alone in the unpainted house with a broken window or two. The yard was slightly grown up with grass and shrubs planted by nature. She lived a secluded life because the majority of neighbors were fearful of her reputation.

Peeking through the window, I was fascinated by a small "stuffed" bird, this being my first glimpse of taxidermy work.

Visits with "Miss Lizzie" were limited to times she would be sweeping her front steps or "stirring" around outside.

Standing out most in my memory of "Miss Lizzie" is that she was among my reliable customers when peddling door-to-door products, such as Rosebud Salve and Flower Seeds. Contributing to our school's paper drive also gained recognition of this friendless woman.

In her little backyard shack, "Miss Lizzie" had what appeared to be every paper she had ever purchased! There were some "Doubting Thomas'" so far as her parting with any of them, but that didn't prevent me from asking.

To the surprise of many, "Miss Lizzie" consented. A classmate and I had a busy time hauling those papers in his little wagon. As a result of her contribution, our class won the award for collecting the most papers for what we know today as recycling.

Here again, another indication that love was present, and enforcement to . . . "the greatest of these is love."

Barking Up The Wrong Tree!

"Barking up the wrong tree," that's what was happening. It took a while to realize it though.

There was something about a particular individual that "bugged" me and much time was devoted in prayer that the situation would change.

Continuous prayer was offered that I would learn to love the other party. My prayers seemed to be in vain. Each time our paths crossed, the dislike for the other party was as great as ever!

Then one Sunday morning during prayer, God planted a thought in my mind that had never been considered. His voice was not heard as your voice or mine when we speak with each other, but He got through to me.

The prayer needed to be offered was for me to be deserving of love from the other party. Take my word for it - Even though no contact was made at the moment, other than prayer, a feeling of contentment and an awareness that things were going to be made right was realized.

As a result of this experience, two people became friends in Christ and each could bear witness that . . . "The greatest of these is love!"

Note: Making the incident above more interesting, is the fact that, today, I could not tell you who the other party is!

Time Heals All Wounds?

The day was no longer than any other, yet seemingly it would never come to an end. Then with darkness, the night lingered on. During the restless hours portions of St. Francis' prayer for the ability to sow joy where there is sadness . . . faith where there is doubt . . . and hope where there is despair, haunted me.

Lacking knowledge of what was to come, my actions had contributed directly to another child of God being hurt. Rather than make a scene with words of accusations, the injured party chose the "route of seclusion."

"Time heals all wounds." Could this famous quotation be applicable in this particular situation? Would the best solution be to wait until time had healed the wounds and the injured party had taken the first step?

In many cases, the best remedy for soothing pain is to allow time. Even so, another famous phrase, "Two wrongs never make a right," repeatedly flashed through my mind.

Then, too, Jesus had said whatever we do to "the least of these", we have done likewise unto Him.

Pondering the incident, putting myself in the other person's place, returning silence for silence seemed wrong. There was only one approach to be taken: that being an outward expression of love. Asking God for guidance and the right opportunity, the waiting period was brief. By not playing the waiting game, the silence was broken.

To say, "I'm sorry" would have been meaningless. To simply say, "I love you" would have been no more meaningful. Love must be shown in order to be sown!

The seriousness of carelessness where others are concerned is often not realized until it is too late.

During our little talk, the injured party commented, "If I had not been afraid that I would go to hell, I would have committed suicide the other night!" A mere comment? Possibly, but pain reflected in the eyes indicated deeper thought.

Thanking God for this person's admission of fear, my prayer was to be instrumental in replacing joy for sadness, faith for doubt, and hope for despair.

A mistake was made and regretted. Reaching out in "brotherly love", the mistake was forgiven in the same spirit. Brotherly love alone is not sufficient however. God's love must be generated in such a way that He will be permitted to take full control of all situations.

Then, and only then, can it truthfully be said that "time heals all wounds." Then, and only then, will the words recorded in I Corinthians 13:13 make such an impression within the heart that it will generate through our thoughts, speech and conduct in our daily living.

From My Heart To Yours

Personal experiences shared through "Reflections", my weekly column in the Houston Home Journal and through this publication are used to briefly summarize how we can learn from our daily experiences.

Living and sharing these experiences has truly enriched my life. I sincerely hope that you, the reader, will be blessed in like manner and we will each be inspired to reflect God's love as we journey through life.

Earline Ross Cole

•••••

50% profit from sales of this book
will be directed to the
Bonaire United Methodist Women
In support of
The BUMC Outreach Ministry

*"Verily I say unto you,
Inasmuch as ye have done it
Unto the least of these my brethren,
Ye have done it unto me."*
--Matthew 25:40b

Thanks!